Your greatest and truest successes
in life come from your reliance on God.

Presented To

_____

Presented By

_____

Date

_____

Each day has twenty-four hours. How you invest those hours is up to you.

SIMPLE LIVING™

for Busy People

SIMPLE LIVING

for Busy People

God's Guide to Enjoying What Matters Most

inspirio

Simple Living for Busy People
ISBN 0-310-80347-0

Copyright © 2004 by GRQ Ink, Inc.
Franklin, Tennessee 37067
"Simple Living" is a trademark owned by GRQ, Inc.

Published by Inspirio™, The gift group of Zondervan
Grand Rapids, Michigan 49530

Requests for information should be addressed to:
Inspirio™, The gift group of Zondervan
5300 Patterson Avenue, SE
Grand Rapids, Michigan 49530
http://www.inspiriogifts.com

Compiler: Lila Empson
Associate Editor: Janice Jacobson
Project Manager: Tom Dean
Manuscript written by Quentin Guy, Jeff Dewsbury, and Rebecca Currington in conjunction with Snapdragon Editorial Group, Inc.
Design: Whisner Design Group, Tulsa, Oklahoma

Printed in China.

03 04 05/HK/ 4 3 2 1

Our culture's preoccupation
with happiness and personal fulfillment
clearly has made us selfish people,
but the worst part of it is
that it hasn't made us happy.

TONY CAMPOLO

Table of Contents

Introduction

Life is complex, and time seems to spin by faster each day. You're tired of feeling squeezed by demands and pressured to go even faster. And you wonder, *Is it possible to live a simpler, more restful life?*

Absolutely—and you can start right now.

Here, forty meditations offer insights and suggestions to help you discover God's gift of inner peace and soul-soothing serenity. So put your feet up. Lean back. Embrace the simple life you dream about.

God does not have a wonderful plan for your life.
He has something far better—
a wonderful purpose.

R. PAUL STEVEN

Saying No

Don't let the good things in life rob you of the best things.
Buster Rothman

Setting and maintaining priorities for your life means saying no as well as saying yes. Saying no to friends, family, coworkers, and charitable organizations can be difficult. But unless you do, other people's priorities will clutter your life and leave you with less time and energy to pursue your own interests.

Saying yes to your boss when he asks you to spend another late night at the office could mean saying no to your son's soccer game or your daughter's dance recital. Agreeing to help with the school bake sale could mean that you miss prayer time or story time with your kids. Saying yes to playing first base for a community softball team could mean saying no to needed rest for your body. Saying yes to a request to chair the paper recycling drive could mean that you give up time to reflect on your life and refresh your soul.

Saying yes to too many good things could mean that you are saying no to your relationship with God. Even when your intentions are the best, those precious times of prayer, Bible

12

reading, and quiet meditation can slip away in the rush of other activities.

If setting priorities were just a matter of putting good things above trivial things, the task would be easy. More often, however, prioritizing is about putting best things ahead of good things and about keeping first things in first place.

Take time to evaluate every new request, project, or activity based on how it will fit in with your priorities. Ask God to help you simplify your life and increase your sense of satisfaction with your decision to simplify.

Read Matthew 6:33 for an excellent guideline for priorities. In the passage where this verse occurs, Jesus was talking to his disciples about how they should live. He urged them to put God things first. Even after two thousand years, that admonition is relevant. When your relationship with God takes first place in your life, he will help you order the rest. As you read the Bible and spend time talking to God in prayer, you will begin to see how all the other pieces of your life fit together.

One Final Thought

Prioritizing your life often means putting best things before good things and keeping first things in first place.

Thoughts for Simply Living

Commit to the LORD everything you do. Then your plans will succeed.

PROVERBS 16:3 NIrV

The surest method of arriving at a knowledge of God's eternal purposes about us is to be found in the right use of the present moment.

FREDERICK WILLIAM FABER

Teach us to count our days that we may gain a wise heart.

PSALM 90:12 NRSV

Give me a person who says, "This one thing I do, and not these fifty things I dabble in."

DWIGHT MOODY

Remember...

_____God has promised to help you establish proper priorities for your life—priorities that truly do put first things first.

_____God can provide wisdom and insight into your motives to help you stay on course.

_____Knowing that your priorities are in place allows you to pursue the tasks before you with enthusiasm and joy.

_____You are the only one who can decide to simplify your life by putting your priorities in order.

Simplify...

Keep a desk calendar so that you can easily see how a request will fit into your schedule.

Before adding something new to your schedule, decide what it will replace.

If you know you can't take something on, say so on the spot.

Schedule specific times for important relationships.

When needed, simply say no; no excuse is necessary.

Every time you make a choice you are turning the central part of you that chooses into something a little different from what it was before.

C. S. LEWIS

Let It Go

Forgiveness is not an occasional art; it is a permanent attitude.
Martin Luther King Jr.

Hanging on to hurt and resentment can be exhausting and painful. Holding a grudge does nothing to undo the offense or ease the pain it caused. The best way to stop the hurting is simply to forgive, without condition.

Breaking through to forgiveness (saying it and actually meaning it) is difficult because it rubs against your humanness. Letting go may feel like you are letting the person who hurt you off the hook, maybe even condoning his or her behavior. The irony is that choosing to forgive lets you off the hook. Forgiveness exchanges a tangled mess of emotion for healing and renewal and releases you to go on with your life.

Forgiveness is tough but possible, especially with God's help. God is the one who established the model for forgiveness, and God practiced it long before you ever had reason to forgive anyone. God created forgiveness as a way of reestablishing relationship with his most cherished creation— humankind.

God doesn't want to see you carrying around a load of

hurt and resentment. He wants you to let go. Things that are impossible for you are possible for him, and miracles happen.

While you're forgiving others, consider the offenses you have committed. Guilt can be as damaging as hurt and resentment. And, once again, forgiveness is the antidote. Acknowledge those things you have done wrong, and ask God to forgive you.

In the course of your earthly life, you will experience times when you need to both give and receive forgiveness. Embrace these times. Make asking and giving forgiveness part of your daily experience. Practice until forgiveness becomes an attitude rather than an action.

Your life will be kinder, gentler, and simpler once you give up the complications caused by unresolved conflict and broken relationships. You may even find yourself feeling light and unfettered, ready to fill up the empty spaces with newfound joy.

One Final Thought

Giving and receiving forgiveness is God's built-in release valve. Don't hold on to hurt, resentment, and guilt. Experience the freedom that comes from letting go.

Thoughts for Simply Living

Bear with one another, and, if anyone has a complaint against another, forgive each other; just as the Lord has forgiven you, so you also must forgive.

COLOSSIANS 3:13 NRSV

To forgive is to set a prisoner free and discover the prisoner was you.

AUTHOR UNKNOWN

Jesus said, "If you forgive others their trespasses, your heavenly Father will also forgive you; but if you do not forgive others, neither will your Father forgive your trespasses."

MATTHEW 5:14–15 NRSV

When you forgive, you in no way change the past—but you sure do change the future.

BERNARD MELTZER

Remember...

_____God has placed the responsibility and privilege for giving and receiving forgiveness in your hands.

_____Forgiveness brings a sense of joy and relief to your life.

_____God has promised to perform a mighty miracle in your heart, freeing you to use your energy in more productive ways.

_____Forgiving others places you in the path of healing and restoration for your own life.

Simplify...

Before you go to sleep at night, forgive those who have offended you and ask for God's forgiveness.

Apologize quickly and specifically when you commit an offense.

For additional help, write the offense on a piece of paper and then tear the paper into tiny pieces, demonstrating your decision to give and receive forgiveness.

Find a quiet place and ask for God's help in learning to forgive.

When you want to forgive, but can't seem to do it, give God time to get your heart lined up with your decision.

We are chained to that which we do not forgive.

RICHARD PAUL EVANS

Lighten the Load

Lives based on having are less free than lives based either
on doing or on being.
William James

Consider how many things you have. Do you have a
storage shed, a basement, or an attic to keep the excess out
of sight? It's quite a chore to store and protect so many
possessions. You've probably wondered why you do it or
what you can do about it.

It's comforting to know you have something for every
occasion. It's comforting to have a backup mower in the
shed waiting to be pushed into action if your new
lawnmower breaks down. And then there's the wicker settee
and rocker you moved up to the attic when you bought the
new sofa and chair. You don't have room for the old
furniture any more, but those pieces were too good to get
rid of.

Consider the ice cream freezer sitting in the garage, used
twice, but still packed in its original box. And how about
the once-used glue gun, boxes and boxes of jigsaw puzzles, a
bicycle you never ride, and a rack of clothes you haven't

been able to wear since you gained thirty pounds. You think, perhaps, that you'll be able to wear them again one day.

The problem with having so much stuff is that somewhere along the line the volume of accumulated possessions begins to take over your life, hogging your space, sapping your peace of mind.

Give yourself a good shake and take charge. Donate those clothes to the nearest Goodwill store or the Salvation Army. Give those puzzles to a retirement center.

The point is that you should be taking control of your things rather than allowing your things to take control of you. You will enjoy a wonderful freedom when you move that mountain of possessions and create a calm, uncluttered space.

God doesn't begrudge you your possessions, but neither does he want you to be so encumbered by them that you lose sight of those treasures that are imperishable—treasures such as spiritual growth and relationships with family and friends.

One Final Thought

Unless you make an effort to control your accumulation of possessions, your possessions will eventually control you.

Thoughts for Simply Living

Jesus said, "Watch out and guard yourselves from every kind of greed; because your true life is not made up of the things you own, no matter how rich you may be."

LUKE 12:15 GNT

It is easier to renounce worldly possessions than it is to renounce the love of them.

WALTER HILTON

Jesus said, "Do not be afraid, little flock, for your Father has been pleased to give you the kingdom. Sell your possessions and give to the poor. Provide purses for yourselves that will not wear out, a treasure in heaven that will not be exhausted, where no thief comes near and no moth destroys. For where your treasure is, there your heart will be also."

LUKE 12:32–34 NIV

He who possesses most must be most afraid of loss.

LEONARDO DA VINCI

Remember...

_____Unlike earthly treasures that will not last, spiritual treasures, such as love, peace, and joy, have eternal value.

_____God can provide wisdom and insight into your motives for obtaining and accumulating possessions.

_____Freeing yourself of unneeded possessions will make it easier to utilize and enjoy the possessions you decide to keep.

_____Sharing those things you can't use with others who can is a warm and enriching experience.

Simplify...

Limit yourself to one storage area.

Look for an organization that could benefit from the stored furniture you no longer use.

Each month, clean and reorganize one closet. Ask a friend to help you make objective choices.

When you fill a box to give away, close it up so you won't be tempted to look inside and reclaim something.

Use the exchange method: Each time you bring something home, give away something to make room for it.

It is not what you have but instead what God has that you have.

G. RAY JORDAN

Going Deeper

It is in the ordinary duties and labors of life that the Christian can
and should develop his spiritual union with God.
                Thomas Merton

You may think you don't have time to build a relationship
with God—simple or otherwise. But opportunities may be
lurking in places you never imagined. In the midst of your busy
life, there are a myriad of mundane "necessary" duties that may
seem insignificant at the time. It's while performing those tasks,
the things you can often do on autopilot, that you have a
chance to build a deeper faith.

Closely examine your household activities for the next
couple of days. Folding the laundry, changing the oil in the car,
loading the dishwasher, cleaning the swimming pool, dusting
the furniture, carrying out the trash—every day offers a wealth
of these times when your hands are busy but your mind and
spirit are free.

While you're mowing the lawn, you may want to hold a
good, old-fashioned prayer session with God. While you're
waiting for the kids to come flooding out of the school and pile
into the car, you may want to read a particular portion of the

Bible, perhaps as part of a systematic Bible reading program. While carrying out your daily exercise regimen, you may want to meditate on a certain scripture or just think about God.

Using these opportunities to grow closer to God can actually bring relief to your busy schedule. Talking things over with God can help you sort through nagging issues and prepare strategies for complicated situations. Frequent Bible reading can provide wisdom and understanding that will help you simplify your life by giving you time to make thoughtful choices for yourself.

While compartmentalizing is a great way to keep your closet neat, relegating your faith to one area of your life isn't quite so tidy. Spread it out to every part of your day and transform those less-than-challenging tasks into living acts of worship and communication with God—a deeper relationship with God is a matter of simple faith.

One Final Thought

You can experience serenity in the midst of your busy life by inviting God into the normal, mundane moments of your day.

Thoughts for Simply Living

That everyone may eat and drink, and find satisfaction
in all his toil—this is the gift of God.

ECCLESIASTES 3:13 NIV

If we place our religious progress in outward observances only, our devotion
will soon come to an end.

THOMAS À KEMPIS

In him we live and move and exist.

ACTS 17:28 NIrV

Nothing is too little to be ordered by our Father; nothing too little in which to
see His hand; nothing which touches our souls too little to accept from Him;
nothing too little to be done to Him.

EDWARD BOUVERIE PUSEY

Remember...

_____Opportunities for developing a closer relationship with God often lurk in unexpected places.

_____Even the boring, humdrum aspects of your day can be fulfilling if you view them as an opportunity to let God speak to you.

_____Part of growing closer to God is simply learning to recognize the sound of his voice in your inner being.

_____The more you allow God into your daily affairs, the easier you will find it to make the most of your busy day.

Simplify...

Each time you perform the task you dislike the most, thank God for a few specific blessings.

Keep a bookmark in your Bible so that you can easily find your place.

Purchase a small paperback version of the Bible to keep in your car to read whenever you have to wait.

Think of a few weekly household tasks to combine with reading or memorizing small portions of Scripture.

Pinpoint a couple of quiet jobs where it will be easiest to keep your own thoughts still and let God speak to you.

Once Christ comes to live in us, he begins to move out into every area of our minds and hearts. He is never finished with us.

LLOYD JOHN OGLIVIE

More than Enough

He who is not content with little will never be satisfied with much.
Thomas Benton Brooks

Everyone has dreams and aspirations. You may long to be well-off financially, to be an influential person in your community, to be a knowledgeable, well-traveled individual. These are all worthwhile goals. They can spell trouble, however, if you shackle yourself to them and disallow yourself any chance to relax and simply enjoy your life.

Have you ever been to a high school or college reunion? Did you feel a little unsettled in the pit of your stomach after seeing a photo of the type of house a classmate lives in or hearing what big achievers his or her children are? That's a perfectly normal response. But comparing yourself to others can motivate you to pursue goals that won't ever satisfy you.

Second Peter 1:5–8 exhorts you to strive to be better, push forward, add to who you are. It's a biblical ideal that says being content isn't the same as resigning yourself or settling for less. A content person can still be driven to succeed, to reach new heights at work, at home, in hobbies, and in personal improvement. But those goals can enrich your life rather than fill it with stress.

Slow down your busy pace for a moment and take a close and honest look at who you are. What God has placed in you, in your daily life—that's what really matters. Consider the elements of your world that make you smile and give you the feeling that life has a lot to offer—kids, cherished friendships, hot baths, and your easy chair.

Contentment comes from looking inward, examining yourself, praising God that he has brought you this far, thanking him for the blessings he has poured out on your life. Let your aspirations take you on a ride high above the clouds, let them motivate you to do great things, let them keep you fired up, living to the max. But refuse to let your aspirations goad you into running a futile, empty race. That's when life starts to feel complicated. Keep it simple.

One Final Thought

Dreams and aspirations are great, but they must be kept in their place—secondary to the simple and remarkable blessings God has placed in your life.

Thoughts for Simply Living

You will keep in perfect peace him whose mind is steadfast, because he trusts in you.

ISAIAH 26:3 NIV

It is so important not to waste what is precious by spending all one's time and emotion on fretting or complaining over what one does not have.

EDITH SCHAEFFER

The fruit of righteousness will be peace; the effect of righteousness will be quietness and confidence forever.

ISAIAH 32:17 NIV

The utmost we can hope for in this life is contentment.

JOSEPH ADDISON

Remember...

_____Contentment comes by looking inward and appreciating the person you really are.

_____Contentment comes by appreciating and enjoying the simple pleasures God has placed in your life.

_____God has given you every tool you could possibly need to achieve contentment in your life.

_____Improving yourself, striving for more is fine as long as you keep those things in proper perspective.

Simplify...

Focus on five things that make you happy to be who you are.

For one day, take a break from radio, television, newspapers, and your computer.

Whenever you find yourself stressed out because you're dreaming about things you don't have, stop and thank God for one good real thing already in your life.

Take a moment before you go to sleep to recall one thing that made you laugh or smile that day.

Bring your needs to God each day. This will free your mind from worry and frustration.

We forget that happiness doesn't come as a result of getting something we don't have, but rather of recognizing and appreciating what we do have.

FREDERICK KEONIG

Simple Living
Simple Faith

Faith is simply believing God; and, like sight, it is nothing apart from its object.

HANNAH WHITALL SMITH

Now that we have been put right with God through faith, we have peace with God through our Lord Jesus Christ.
ROMANS 5:1 GNT

Faith is the assurance of things hoped for, the conviction of things not seen.
HEBREWS 11:1 NRSV

The Scripture says, "The person who is put right with God through faith shall live."
ROMANS 1:17 GNT

Doubt sees the obstacles;
Faith sees the way.
Doubt sees the darkest night;
Faith sees the day.
Doubt dreads to take a step;
Faith soars on high.
Doubt questions, "Who believes?"
Faith answers, "I."

AUTHOR UNKNOWN

Just Say It

Little keys can open big locks. Simple words can express great thoughts.
William Arthur Ward

When it comes to speech, it's often true that less is more. It is a good thing to keep your speech simple, direct, and uncluttered with innuendo and hidden agendas. Once you've succeeded in simplifying your speech, you'll find that other aspects of your life are simpler as well. You will have fewer misunderstandings, fewer relational problems, and fewer jobs that have to be redone.

You can simplify your speaking habits by remembering a few easy concepts. First, always speak to others as equals before God. Even if you're an expert on the topic (especially if you are), find ways to get your main points across without sounding superior or condescending. Keep in mind that the person you are speaking to lacks information rather than intelligence.

Try also to avoid jargon, especially when speaking to others about God. Jesus didn't use jargon when he spoke. Keep your conversation free of clutter, and you will have a better chance of making your point.

Another key to simplifying your conversation is to make eye contact with the person to whom you are speaking. Use simple sentences when giving instructions or directions.

Let your yes be yes and your no be no. Say what you mean and mean what you say. People are more apt to listen to what you have to say if they know your words can be trusted.

Imagine how much better, how much simpler your life would be if you could communicate with others and they understood you the first time. Wouldn't it be nice if you only had to give instructions one time?

You're a busy person—too busy to have to repeatedly explain an unclear communication. Make your speech simple and direct, and your life will follow suit.

One Final Thought

Keeping your words honest and direct will help you communicate more effectively and avoid confusion, misunderstandings, and other obstacles to a simple life.

Thoughts for Simply Living

The heart of the righteous ponders how to answer.
PROVERBS 15:28 NASB

Speaking without thinking is shooting without aiming.
SIR WILLIAM GURNEY BENHAM

What a joy it is to find just the right word for
the right occasion!
PROVERBS 15:23 GNT

When you have nothing to say, say nothing.
CHARLES CALEB COLTON

Remember...

_____God can help you learn to keep your speech uncluttered.

_____God wants you to speak honestly and truthfully because it keeps your heart unfettered.

_____Conflict can be avoided when others know that your words can be trusted.

_____God's words to you are a model; they are always simple and direct.

Simplify...

Wait until you have heard what the other person has to say before formulating a response.

> Write out instructions before you present them to ensure that they are clear.

If you are uncertain about whether you should say something about a certain issue, choose to say nothing.

> When speaking of Jesus, season your words so that they are tasty and easy to digest.

Read the book of Proverbs and mark the verses that have to do with controlling your speech.

Ideal conversation must be an exchange of thought, and not, as many of those who worry most about their shortcomings believe, an eloquent exhibition of wit or oratory.

EMILY POST

Time for People

A relationship is a living thing. It needs and benefits from the same attention to detail that an artist lavishes on his art.
David Viscott

*P*lacing your relationships at the top of your daily list of activities and spending time to nurture those relationships can help you simplify your life by helping you stay focused on what is truly important—people. Determine each day to keep your relationships in the forefront of your life.

Once you've determined to always put people first, a good place to start is with your relationship with God. This vital relationship set the stage for keeping all your other relationships strong. God is the one who understands you best and the one who has brought the people you love into your life. Spending time with him will make you more sensitive and caring. You will need his help to give you the strength and consistency to reach out to those you love consistently.

If you are married, your spouse is the next person who should have your attention each day. This is the person to whom you have committed your life in a covenant relationship before God. There are great rewards for finding fresh, new ways to express your love and devotion each day, including a more harmonious home environment free of misunderstandings.

If you have children, they also need your time and attention. Finding time to spend with each one each day can be a challenge, but doing so helps to keep the lines of communication open and family expectations clear.

Your family of origin—parents, siblings, and other relatives—deserve your attention as well, as do your close friends. Take time on a regular basis to nurture deep relationships. They will help you stay balanced, provide good advice, and help you avoid making costly choices outside your home.

Taking time for the people in your life, daily nurturing those most important relationships, can bring you much closer to a simple, harmonious lifestyle.

One Final Thought

Putting time with the people at the top of your list of activities will help you stay focused on what is really important as you strive to simplify your life.

Thoughts for Simply Living

How good and how pleasant it is for brethren to dwell together in unity.

PSALM 133:1 KJV

Use your head to handle yourself, your heart to handle others.

AUTHOR UNKNOWN

Do nothing from selfishness or empty conceit, but with humility of mind regard one another as more important than yourselves.

PHILIPPIANS 2:3 NASB

Constant kindness can accomplish much. As the sun makes ice melt, kindness causes misunderstanding, mistrust and hostility to evaporate.

ALBERT SCHWEITZER

Remember...

_____When you spend time with God, he will give you insights about how to spend more time with the people in your life.

_____Jesus always put people upfront and center in his life.

_____Solid friendships bring balance and other important resources to your life.

_____Each day has twenty-four hours. How you invest those hours is up to you.

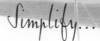

Simplify...

Actively seek quality in your relationships, shoring up where necessary.

Pursue transparency by letting others see who you really are.

At the beginning of each week, specifically plan an activity with each member of your family, even if it's something as simple as running errands together.

Pray for wisdom and discernment as you strive to keep proper boundaries in your relationships.

Release yourself from toxic or unbalanced relationships that steal your time and sanity.

*Reinforce the stitch that ties us,
and I will do the same for you.*

DORIS SCHERIN

God's Purpose

God is the only goal worthy of men's efforts; the fitting end of human existence is a loving union with God.

Saint Augustine of Hippo

God has a plan and purpose for your life—a purpose that fits perfectly with the gifts and talents he has placed in you. When your goals are in harmony with God's plan, your life is bound to be simpler and happier.

The concept that God has created you with a specific purpose in mind may make perfect sense to you, and yet you wonder how to identify and get into step with that purpose. Some important principles can get you on track, help you with your goal-setting, and make that process easier.

Set a goal to spend time getting to know your Creator. Choose a time each day to read a chapter from the New Testament—before bed is a great time. Soon you will begin to understand more about who God is and his overall intentions for humankind. In addition to your reading, spend time talking to God. He is listening. Speak to him throughout your busy day—while you're waiting in traffic, walking to an appointment, or waiting to see someone.

42

Next, set a goal to spend time getting to know yourself. God has placed gifts and talents in your life—some are obvious and some are waiting to be discovered. Make a list of activities and tasks you're good at and enjoy. Note what makes you feel happy and motivated.

As you discover more and more about God and about yourself, you will find it easier to set goals that are consistent with who you really are and what you are meant to do and be. You may learn that God has called you to care for others. You may discover that God has endowed you with a gift of patience with people, a knack for communicating, and the ability to encourage and motivate people. Realizing that God has called and equipped you for a particular profession, you will need to set goals to obtain the needed expertise.

One Final Thought

The key to simplifying your life in regard to goals is to set wise, clear, and attainable goals consistent with God's purpose for your life.

Thoughts for Simply Living

We make it our goal to please him.
2 CORINTHIANS 5:9 NIV

No one can be making much of his life who has not a very definite conception of what he is living for.

HENRY DRUMMOND

Jesus said, "Seek first his kingdom and his righteousness, and all these things will be given to you as well."
MATTHEW 6:33 NIV

Aim at heaven and you will get earth thrown in. Aim at earth and you will get neither.

C. S. LEWIS

Remember...

_____Your goals should be aimed at helping you fulfill the purpose for which you were created.

_____God desires to reveal his purpose for your life as you get to know him better.

_____The gifts and talents God has given you are always in harmony with God's purpose for you.

_____Goals are much easier to attain when you know that what you do pleases God.

Simplify...

Determine to read one chapter from the New Testament each day for insight into God's purposes.

Evaluate your present goals. Are they consistent with your innate gifts and talents?

Through prayer, get to know God better and listen down deep inside for wisdom concerning his purpose for your life.

Set attainable goals that are specific and time-phased.

When setting goals, be true to the vision God has given you—even if you only have one or two pieces of the puzzle.

God does not have a wonderful plan for your life. He has something far better—a wonderful purpose.

R. PAUL STEVEN

Real Treasure

All the wealth of the world cannot be compared to
living together happily united.
Saint Margaret d'Youville

Your family may be the reason you have set out on this
quest to simplify your life. Perhaps you are longing to have
more time to spend with them. That's a wonderful
motivation—and a wonderful resource. Make your family
part of goal to simplify and your chances for success will
greatly increase.

Replace one activity in your schedule for time alone
with a family member at least once a week. That may mean
foregoing an hour of television or giving up your place on
the bowling league. It could mean reading one less chapter
in your novel or choosing not to bring work home from the
office. Let love for your family help you cut back your
schedule by identifying those activities you can live without.

Invite family members to join you in pursuit of a
simpler lifestyle. Consider making this a rule: each family
member is to address each of the others with respect as
fitting a person created in the image of God. This rule could

improve family relations by minimizing time wasted dealing with disputes, hurt feelings, anger, and resentment.

Another rule might be this: each family member must speak truthfully at all times. Rejecting dishonesty helps to eliminate complications, the tangled webs that are woven when the truth is not valued.

Consider rules that encourage respect for personal space and property as well. Address issues such as division of family responsibilities. When your list is complete, set aside a special time to review the rules, adjust them according to family member input, and pray over them.

Family members might work together to create a list of general tips for simplifying family life. These can be as basic as rules to come to the dinner table on time, do homework before watching television, and begin each meal with prayer.

You and your loved ones can create any environment you want in your home if you work together.

One Final Thought

Your family is a wonderful motivator and a great resource.
Work together to make a simple life a reality.

Thoughts for Simply Living

If someone does not know how to manage his own
household, how can he take care of God's church?
1 TIMOTHY 3:5 NRSV

If you wish your children to be Christians you must really take the trouble to be Christians yourselves. Those are the only terms upon which the home will work the gracious miracle.

WOODROW WILSON

God sets the lonely in families.
PSALM 68:6 NIV

Pray together and read the Bible together. Nothing strengthens a marriage and family more. Nothing is a better defense against Satan.

BILLY GRAHAM

Remember...

_____Your family is precious—they are a gift from God.

_____God wants you to work together to create the simple lifestyle you long for.

_____God created the universe to move in harmony. He has designed your family to live in harmony as well.

_____God is the most important person in your family. He can bring insight and wisdom to your family endeavors.

Simplify...

Set an example by being willing to replace expendable activities for family time.

> Set aside one meal a week for family discussion about how to achieve and maintain a simple lifestyle.

Pray that God will help each family member separate the important from the unnecessary.

> Read from the Gospels about the simple life of Jesus; list what Jesus included in his life and what he eliminated.

Encourage family members to submit to one another.

I wondered—not for the first time—whether one was ever justified in neglecting the welfare of one's own family in order to fight for the welfare of others.

NELSON MANDELA

A Simple Perspective

Change your thoughts and you change your world.
Norman Vincent Peale

You can do many things to simplify your busy life—you can communicate more effectively, disciple yourself, and organize your home and schedule, to name a few. For success in achieving your goal, however, you will need to do more than make changes in your behavior. You will have to change your thinking.

Your thoughts have a great deal to do with your success in any goal you may set for your life. That's because, to a large extent, your mind controls your body. You are in change.

The best way to control your thoughts is to control what you put into your mind. When you feed your thoughts the positive food it needs, you will be able to better define your real desires, clarify what course of action you need to take, and motivate yourself to push past obstacles and stick to your efforts until your goal becomes a reality.

If your goal is to slow down, get rid of the clutter in your life, and lead a more peaceful existence, then you must determine to feed your thoughts with input that will help you get there.

Read in the Gospels about the life Jesus led. He cared little for earthly possessions, had strong relationships with close friends, and spoke in a direct manner. His life was focused on doing the will of his father in heaven.

Observe the everyday lives of people who have chosen a simpler way of life. Note attitudes and actions that have helped that person live in the way he or she chooses.

Read articles that offer tips and benefits about the simple life.

As you choose appropriate food for your thoughts, you will feel more and more motivated to undertake and stick with the activities and actions that will lead you to success in your pursuit.

Your mind is a gift from God, designed to help you reach the goals you set for your life. Make sure your mind is working for you as you seek a simple life.

One Final Thought

To effectively simplify your life, you must first change your thinking by putting the right things into your mind.

Thoughts for Simply Living

Whatever is true, whatever is noble, whatever is right, whatever is pure, whatever is lovely, whatever is admirable—if anything is excellent or praiseworthy—think about such things.

PHILIPPIANS 4:8 NIV

A Christian is a person who thinks in believing and believes in thinking.

SAINT AUGUSTINE OF HIPPO

Do not conform any longer to the pattern of this world, but be transformed by the renewing of your mind. Then you will be able to test and approve what God's will is—his good, pleasing and perfect will.

ROMANS 12:2 NIV

As soon as man does not take his existence for granted, but beholds it as something unfathomably mysterious, thought begins.

ALBERT SCHWEITZER

Remember...

_____Your mind is a gift from God, designed to help you in your endeavor to make your life simpler.

_____God has given you the power to decide what type of input you want to put into your mind

_____God can provide the insights and wisdom you need to make your goal of a simpler life possible.

_____The clearer your mind, the better you will be able to accomplish your goal to simplify your mind.

Simplify...

Commit to rid yourself of all useless activities that lead to mental pollution.

Figure out what your worries and fears are, then put them in God's hands and leave them there.

Refresh your mind by choosing positive, uplifting entertainment.

When you read the Bible, think about what God is saying and how you can live it.

Discipline your mind to imitate Jesus' characteristics of humility, servanthood, gentleness, and patience.

You are today where your thoughts have brought you; you will be tomorrow where your thoughts take you.

JAMES ALLEN

Simple Living
Simple Love

Love seeks one thing only:
the good of the one loved.

THOMAS MERTON

You shall love the LORD *your God*
with all your heart, and with all your
soul, and with all your might.
DEUTERONOMY 6:5 NRSV

Jesus said, "I give you a new
commandment, that you love one
another. Just as I have loved you, you
also should love one another."
JOHN 13:34 NRSV

If I speak in the tongues of mortals
and of angels, but do not have love,
I am a noisy gong or a clanging
cymbal.
1 CORINTHIANS 13:1 NRSV

Beloved, let us love
For love is light,
And he who loveth not
Dwelleth in night.

Beloved, let us love
For only thus
Shall we behold that God
Who loveth us.

HORATIUS BONAR

All in Good Time

Fulfillment of your destiny does not come in a moment, a month, or a year, but over a lifetime.
Casey Treat

God has a plan and a purpose for your life. Jeremiah 29:11–12 (NIV) says, "'I know the plans I have for you,' declares the LORD, 'plans to prosper you and not to harm you, plans to give you hope and a future. Then you will call upon me and come and pray to me, and I will listen to you. You will seek me and find me when you seek me with all your heart.'" That's why your sense of fulfillment comes only from him. Trying to find meaning for your life in any other way will only result in confusion and frustration.

Look for a moment at the life of Mother Teresa. That extraordinary woman chose a single room in which to dwell. She had few or no possessions. She spent her time caring for the poor, the sick, and the dying. A busy life? Very. Calcutta provided no shortage of suffering human beings. A simple life? Definitely. Hers was a life reduced to the bare necessities. A fulfilled life? Certainly. Mother Teresa often stated that she found great fulfillment in following the plan God had outlined for her life.

Whatever God has planned for you will be wonderful. It will be right. It will be just exactly what you were created to do. How will you find that one wonderful thing that God has for you? By listening as he speaks to you deep down inside and following in the path where he leads you. Your heart will let you know you're headed in the right direction.

If you have been rushing through life, searching for something that will bring you satisfaction, spend time reading the Bible. Ask God to lead you in the right direction and then listen for his voice.

As his plan unfolds, all the striving to find yourself will end, and you will find yourself on a path of peaceful simplicity. You probably won't be asked to reduce your life as drastically as Mother Teresa did, but you will know that all you really need is that which is necessary to fulfill God's will and purpose.

One Final Thought

God has a plan for your life that will fulfill you in every way.
You will find it only by finding him.

Thoughts for Simply Living

Jesus said, "Blessed are they which do hunger and thirst after righteousness: for they shall be filled."

MATTHEW 5:7 KJV

Find satisfaction in him who made you, and only then find satisfaction in yourself as part of his creation.

SAINT AUGUSTINE OF HIPPO

The LORD will fulfill his purpose for me; your love, O LORD, endures forever—do not abandon the works of your hands.

PSALM 138:8 NIV

Do not give your heart to that which does not satisfy your heart.

ABBA POEMEN

Remember...

_____God has a wonderful plan for your life, and he is eager to help you discover it.

_____A true sense of fulfillment comes only from discovering and pursuing God's plan.

_____God has his own standard for success, which is to fulfill the purpose for which you were created.

_____All God requires is a listening ear, an open heart, and feet that are quick to follow his lead.

Simplify...

Study the words of Jesus to learn about God's will and purpose for his life.

Schedule time each day to seek God in prayer concerning his purpose and plan for your life.

Set aside all preconceived ideas about what God has in store for you.

Take it slow. God will reveal his plan in his perfect time.

Determine to enjoy the life God has given you one day, one step at a time.

Our culture's preoccupation with happiness and personal fulfillment clearly has made us selfish people, but the worst part of it is that it hasn't made us happy.

TONY CAMPOLO

The Master Key

God does not discipline us to subdue us, but to condition us for a life of usefulness and blessedness.
Billy Graham

The word discipline refers to the rules needed to gain and maintain order. In terms of lifestyle issues, it often inspires images of obligation and restriction. The truth is, discipline can lead to liberation, enhanced productivity, and a happier, simpler way of life.

Exercising personal discipline puts you in the driver's seat of your life. It allows you to set the pace. By initiating certain routines, you can lessen the time and energy expended when it is necessary to make the same decisions day after day. You will be able to schedule your time more efficiently and even combine certain activities.

Setting aside a particular time each day for prayer and Bible reading will help you avoid the guilt and frustration that comes from trying to fit God into your already bursting schedule.

Think about it this way. You've decided to plant a small garden behind your house. You first till the ground. You loosen the soil evenly, dividing your plot into rows. Once you prepare the soil, you take one packet of seeds at a time and sprinkle them evenly along the row—one type of vegetable per row. You then commit yourself to tend the garden, watering and weeding regularly.

Now imagine what would happen if you shoveled up the dirt and threw the seeds into the soil any way they happened to fall rather than discipline yourself to plant them evenly down the rows. You would soon have a garden growing out of control. And what if you decided to water and weed only when you really felt like it rather than disciplining yourself to tend your garden each day?

Pause for a moment to think about your busy life. Do you have daily routines? Do you avoid marginal results by seeking to make your routines more effective? Make discipline your friend. Embrace it and put it to work simplifying your life.

One Final Thought

Discipline increases your freedom, cuts the waste from your life, and allows you to choose where you will spend your time and energy.

Thoughts for Simply Living

I discipline my body and make it my slave, so that, after I
have preached to others, I myself will not be disqualified.

1 CORINTHIANS 9:27 NASB

The best discipline, maybe the only discipline that really works,
is self-discipline.

WALTER KIECHEL III

Like a city that is broken into and without walls
is a man who has no control over his spirit.

PROVERBS 25:28 NASB

You will never be the person you can be if pressure, tension,
and discipline are taken out of your life.

JAMES G. BILKEY

Remember...

_____Through discipline, God can help you effectively use your time and energy.

_____Knowing when to say "Bring it on!" and when to say "Enough" are key components of disciplined work habits.

_____Discipline starts with small steps: one Bible chapter, five minutes for prayer, three minutes for making your bed and straightening your room.

_____Your greatest and truest successes in life come from your reliance on God.

Simplify...

Set aside time each morning to plan your day.

Be on time. Doing what it takes to get there promptly develops discipline.

Take a proactive approach to life: plan, set goals, organize.

Make the time for what you value.

Control your spending. Avoid unplanned shopping trips or borrowing money on impulse.

Discipline becomes a means of grace through which God works and moves to transform.

M. ROBERT MULHOLLAND

Everything in Its Place

All things should be done decently and in order.
1 Corinthians 14:40 NRSV

Organizing your home can be a valuable key to simplifying your life. Organization involves setting up a structure for order, such as having a place for everything.

Designating a place for your keys or keeping the mail in one place can help to alleviate confusion and stress. Imagine how much time you could save if the car keys were always handy when you were ready to leave. Keeping the mail in one place ensures that you will not overlook or misplace important papers, letters, or bills that arrive.

This principle also extends to other items in your home. Keeping your medications in one place will help ensure that they stay out of reach of children. A grocery list stuck to the refrigerator will help you remember all the items you need at the supermarket and cut down on return trips. Keeping a dry-erase calendar where family members can record upcoming activities will keep you from missing important events and double booking. Organizational tricks such as these help you avoid stress and conflict and make your life much simpler.

Psalm 136 says that God, by his understanding, created the universe. He created a structure of order for the heavens, setting in place an ingenious operating system for the sun, the stars, the planets, and their moons.

Jesus also demonstrated organization in his earthly ministry. When he instructed his disciples to feed more than five thousand hungry people with a small boy's lunch, he asked the people to sit on the ground in groups. The disciples were told to move through the crowds in an orderly manner, distributing the food from baskets.

Getting organized may sound like more work—something else to crowd into your busy schedule. But establishing a structure of order in your home takes little time and can pay off in a simpler and more pleasant lifestyle for you as well as for everyone who depends on you.

One Final Thought

Organization is a tool for you to use—an important tool that will save you time and steps in your quest to simplify your life.

Thoughts for Simply Living

The plans of the diligent lead surely to abundance.
PROVERBS 21:5 NRSV

Dig the well before you are thirsty.
ANCIENT PROVERB

Prepare your minds for action; be self-controlled;
set your hearts fully on the grace to be given you
when Jesus Christ is revealed.
1 PETER 1:13 NIV

Good order is the foundation of all good things.
EDMUND BURKE

Remember...

_____Organization is a simple skill rather than a gift or talent. You are able to use it as little or as much as you see fit.

_____God provided an example for organization by setting the universe in motion according to an orderly pattern.

_____Organization helps you to make the most of the time and energy God has given you.

_____The order that organization brings can free you to use more of your resources in the way God intended them to be used.

Simplify...

Use a day planner or a desk calendar to help you organize your activities.

Designate a place for the mail, the car keys, important papers, and messages.

Create a list of important addresses and phone numbers and keep it in a desk drawer where you can find it.

Find a safe place for all your medications. It should be a convenient place but out of the reach of children.

If you regularly bring home work from the office, designate a place to work and keep all your work papers in that one place.

The earth as God created it is a masterpiece of organization. He must have known that order is an environment in which we would thrive.

ANDREA GARVEY

Throw Away Your Pride

Just as darkness retreats before light, so all anger and bitterness disappear before the fragrance of humility.
Saint John Climacus

Pursue humility. A humble heart is unclouded by the complexity of self-serving endeavors. Imagine—no more competing for the top rung on the ladder, no more jockeying for position, no more wrestling for credit or defending your actions and behaviors.

A humble heart puts the fun back in basketball night at church and in the company softball league. It drains the power from office politics and neighborhood one-upmanship. Best of all, it helps you enjoy your life with the people you love.

Humility makes a difference in your life because it is more than a behavior or an action. It is an attitude that penetrates to the root of your being. It is a change that takes place inside of you. The corporate ladder is no longer an issue because your humble heart urges you to let God set the pace for your life. Relationships are improved because you no longer feel the urge to always be right. You are able to forego taking the credit for any particular achievement because your humble heart reminds you that God enables you in all you do.

Humility is the hallmark of those who have risen above human definitions of position and status. When you are truly humble, you have discovered how much you are worth. You can choose to place others ahead of yourself. No more struggling to get others to value you as they should.

The best place to seek a humble heart is the Bible. The life of Jesus Christ is a model of humility. Though he was the only Son of God, Jesus laid down the benefits of his position and power. He gave himself freely to mankind, looking only to God to defend his honor. Your humble heart will come in the same way—as you surrender your rights and privileges in the service of others.

Follow the example Jesus set. You will find yourself free from the expectations of others, which is a prelude to a simpler life, a more relaxed approach to living.

One Final Thought

Humility will relieve you of the obligation to promote your own self interests, thereby eliminating the need to strive to prove yourself to others.

Thoughts for Simply Living

Jesus said, "All who exalt themselves will be humbled, and those who humble themselves will be exalted."

LUKE 14:11 NRSV

For those who would learn God's ways, humility is the first thing, humility is the second, humility is the third.

SAINT AUGUSTINE OF HIPPO

"This is the one to whom I will look, to the humble and contrite in spirit, who trembles at my word," says the LORD.

ISAIAH 66:2 NRSV

If you are humble, nothing will touch you, neither praise nor disgrace, because you know what you are.

MOTHER TERESA

Remember...

_____Mercy and grace are your bywords to help you remember your position before God and to help you cultivate a humble servant's spirit.

_____The prospect of eternal life allows you to move past the temporal offerings of this world to receive the choice blessings of spending eternity with God.

_____Your greatest joy will come from the time you spend seeking to bring joy into others' lives.

_____Humility allows you to rightly identify those things that are truly important in life.

Simplify...

Learn to listen when others speak to you rather focus on what you want to say.

Admit your mistakes rather than ignoring or denying misdeeds.

Put others, regardless of their social standing, ahead of yourself, thereby eliminating the struggle to have others regard you more highly.

As you pray for those who treat you badly, you will find your heart growing humble.

Surrender your aspirations and ambitions to God.

Humility is the sure evidence of Christian virtues.

FRANÁOIS, DUC DE LA ROCHEFOUCAULD

71

Talking It Over

Marriage is like twirling a baton, turning handsprings, or eating with chopsticks; it looks so easy till you try it.
Helen Rowland

Marriage is a gift—a gift from God and a gift you give each other. Tackling life as a married couple can be a challenge. It is a challenge that is not only worth the effort, but it is also one that can make life more fulfilling for you and your spouse.

Communication is one of the most important keys to a good marriage. When it comes to simplifying your married life, the rule is that the more you communicate the better. Even the most basic transfer of information is important because it helps you avoid missed connections and misunderstandings. But another, deeper type of communication has even more potential for helping you create a simpler lifestyle for yourselves: taking time to share your feelings, your thoughts, your hopes, and your dreams.

Talking things over can draw you closer together, help you know each other better, and give your marriage a renewed sense of solidarity. As you submit your thoughts and ideas, even your dilemmas, to each other, you will be able to give and receive valuable insights.

When you communicate your hopes and dreams, you have the advantage of mutual encouragement and shared resources. The Bible says in Ecclesiastes 4:9: "Two are better than one, because they have a good return for their work" (NIV).

While you talk things over, take a few moments to talk with God together. Your special time will be even more valuable as you submit your thoughts, feelings, and plans to God and receive his wisdom.

Your talks can take as little as ten minutes each day. Set aside time right before you go to bed at night to talk over the day. Or you may prefer to spend your time in the morning before your day begins.

Communication takes time, but soon you will see that better communication can eliminate many of the frustrations that complicate your lives together.

One Final Thought

A few minutes spent talking things over each day can strengthen your marriage and simplify your life by helping you work together as a team and avoid misunderstandings.

Thoughts for Simply Living

My mouth will speak words of wisdom; the utterance from my heart will give understanding.

PSALM 49:3 NIV

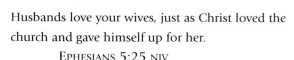

A happy marriage is a long conversation that seems all too short.

ANDRE MAUROIS

Husbands love your wives, just as Christ loved the church and gave himself up for her.

EPHESIANS 5:25 NIV

No pleasure has any savor for me without communication.

MICHEL DE MONTAIGNE

Remember...

_____God created marriage to be a wonderful collaboration between two separate people.

_____Talking things over can help you clarify what is in your own heart and mind.

_____God intends for you to work together as a team, which can multiply your efforts.

_____God is eager to help you in your efforts to communicate more deeply, improve your marriage, and simplify your lives.

Simplify...

Set aside a specific time each day to talk about your feelings, thoughts, hopes, and dreams.

Take a few minutes each morning to clarify who will be responsible for which tasks.

Determine to begin and end your talk time with prayer.

Spend as much time listening to as well as talking with the other.

Determine to see your spouse as someone whose insights can help you pursue a simpler life.

A successful marriage is an edifice that must be rebuilt every day.

ANDRE MAUROIS

75

Simple Living
Simple Hope

Hope is the struggle of the soul, breaking loose from what is perishable, and attesting her eternity.

HERMAN MELVILLE

Find rest, O my soul, in God alone; my hope comes from him.
PSALM 62:5 NIV

May the God of hope fill you with all joy and peace as you trust in him, so that you may overflow with hope by the power of the Holy Spirit.
ROMANS 15:13 NIV

Happy are those whose help is the God of Jacob, whose hope is in the LORD their God.
PSALM 146:5 NRSV

Hope, like the gleaming taper's light

Adorns and cheers our way;

And still, as darker grows the night,

Emits a brighter ray.

OLIVER GOLDSMITH

Forget the Ladder

To love what you do and feel that it matters—how could anything be more fun?
Katharine Graham

Finding simplicity in your work life may require little more than adopting a new perspective on the way you look at what you do.

Until now, you may have been viewing work as an end in itself. This can leave you in a confusing state of flux on any given workday. When things go well, you're riding the crest of the wave, but when they go wrong, you may feel frustrated and dissatisfied. Instead, determine to view your work as an important avenue for identifying and exercising the gifts and talents God has placed in you.

Changing your perspective in this way can free you to work at a level where you feel comfortable, which is better than letting cultural expectations compel you to move up the corporate ladder into a position for which you're not suited. Seeing your job duties as a way of pleasing God and thanking him for all he's given you can help you remain content even when performing the most menial tasks.

Your God-given destiny may include being the man or woman at the top. Life will be simpler if you know God has placed you in your position. Believing your success is the result of human alliances and relationships, or even of your own savvy, puts the weight of maintaining your position and status on you. A sense of peaceful security reigns when you know God is backing you up, providing wisdom and favor, and helping you do your job in a way that is pleasing to him.

Ask God to help identify what he would like to see you accomplish through your employment. You can then make decisions about position changes, promotions, and new responsibilities on the basis of your agenda.

You have the power to maximize the satisfaction you receive from your work and shed confusing expectations imposed by the corporate system. Choose to let your work confirm who you are rather than define it.

One Final Thought

The attitudes with which you approach your work can greatly simplify the role it plays in your life.

Thoughts for Simply Living

Whatever you do, work at it with all your heart, as working
for the Lord, not for men, since you know you will receive
an inheritance from the Lord as a reward.

COLOSSIANS 3:23 NIV

Work is, or should be, the full expression of the worker's faculties, the thing in
which he finds spiritual, mental, and bodily satisfaction, and the medium in
which he offers himself to God.

DOROTHY LEIGH SAYERS

There are varieties of gifts, but the same Spirit, and
there are varieties of services, but the same Lord.

1 CORINTHIANS 12:4 NRSV

When I have learned to do the Father's will, I shall have fully realized my
vocation on earth.

CARLO CARRETTO

Remember...

_____Your work is what you do, not who you are.

_____God's sovereign hand guides your career path just as surely as it does every other aspect of your life.

_____All God expects from you is that you do your best.

_____Pray for strength equal to your tasks. God will help you do what must be done.

Simplify...

List your career objectives and bring them before God in prayer.

Evaluate your objectives in regard to the gifts and talents God has placed in you.

As you prepare for work each day, pray that God will help you accomplish his purposes for you for that day.

Discuss with your employer your personal strengths and areas where you would like to grow.

Determine to let the quality of your work speak for you in the workplace.

A person's vocation is where his or her gifts and passions meet the world's needs.

FREDERICK BUECHNER

Make It a Habit

A man there was, though some did count him mad, the more he cast away, the more he had.
John Bunyan

Becoming a habitual giver is a good way to pursue a simpler lifestyle. Once you have developed a system and schedule for giving, you will find many benefits pertinent to your effort to simplify your life.

One of the ways that giving allows you to simplify your life is by providing an avenue for unloading possessions you no longer want or need. Habitual giving simplifies that process. The more donations you make, the better the process works. Drop-off sites, pickup dates, and appropriate items for donations will become a matter of routine. You will soon discover which organizations can be trusted to make the most of your gifts. Giving regularly greatly simplifies the effort.

Giving helps you simplify by turning your eyes from the superficial assessment of social status—keeping up with the Joneses, for instance—to the value of reaching out to those in need. Giving regularly will help you gain a stronger awareness of the needs around you. The people to whom you give will become more than faces in the crowd. They will be people you have come to know and care about.

Once giving has become an established part of your life and your character, giving yourself to God will be also become simpler. You will find that it is easier to release your burdens to him, surrender your hopes and dreams to him, and give him the love and respect he deserves. All aspects of your life will become more basic and less complex.

Giving will help you get into step with God and with those around you. And if you let it, it will soon become a comfortable habit that benefits you and everyone you touch. Determine to make your giving an often-time event. Make it a regular part of your life. Soon you will know that you can live with less and appreciate what you have more.

One Final Thought

Establishing a habit of giving helps you do more than lighten your load of possessions. It enhances and simplifies your relationship with God, with others, and with the world around you.

Thoughts for Simply Living

Some give freely, yet grow all the richer; others withhold what is due, and only suffer want.

PROVERBS 11:24 NRSV

If you are not generous with a meager income, you will never be generous with abundance.

HAROLD NYE

You should each give, then, as you have decided, not with regret or out of a sense of duty; for God loves the one who gives gladly.

2 CORINTHIANS 9:7 GNT

Nothing is really ours until we share it.

C. S. LEWIS

Remember...

_____God is a habitual giver, giving love, grace, favor, wisdom, and eternal life to all who have need.

_____God encourages you to give because it allows him to pour out his blessings on you.

_____Giving helps you to take your eyes off yourself and to look to the needs of others.

_____Giving makes you more like God, for he is a boundless giver.

Simplify...

Become familiar with the organizations in your area that minister to the needs of others.

Find out what types of donations certain organizations accept.

Plan to donate to at least three organizations on a regular basis; this will give you a recurring avenue for benevolence.

Set some money aside to help out when you see a need.

For two hours a month, give of yourself by visiting someone who is sick or elderly to gain a better awareness of the needs around you.

Somewhere along the way, we must learn that there is nothing greater than to do something for others.

MARTIN LUTHER KING JR.

Pursuing Wholeness

To be "whole" is to be spiritually, emotionally, and physically healthy.
Jesus lived in perfect wholeness.
Colin Urquhart

Wellness—the blessing of a healthy body, mind, and spirit—is an important factor in a simpler lifestyle. Good health frees you to make the most of your life without the complications that illness brings.

Regularly exercise your body, your mind, and your spirit to stay healthy. Evaluate your current activities and aim for balance. If you are working out at the gym, playing softball, and walking five miles each day, you may want to exchange the softball league for a good book or prayer time. Or you can expand a current activity by adding another element to it— praying as you take your five-mile walk, for instance.

Maintaining a healthy diet is another key to staying healthy. Moderation is the key, that is, eating a variety of foods in moderate amounts. God has placed vital nutrients in the myriad foods he has provided. A well-rounded diet will help you receive a good balance of the vitamins and minerals, carbohydrates, fiber, fats, and proteins that your body needs.

Nourishing your mind is also part of a moderate lifestyle. Choose reading materials that offer positive, inspiring messages. Your spiritual diet should include regular doses of prayer and Bible reading.

Because you are a busy person, you may have pushed aside your body's need for rest. Every muscle and nerve in your physical body needs rest to restore itself from the rigors of daily living. Your mind also needs to settle into a relaxed state on a regular basis in order to perform at its peak.

It's essential to find time to let God bring rest and restoration to your spirit. No matter how busy you are, set aside a few moments to go over your day with God. Seek his company and let your spirit relax in the warmth of his presence.

Pursuing good physical, mental, and spiritual health will require time and focus at first, but it is an effective investment that promises worthwhile dividends in your quest for a simple life.

One Final Thought

Health—physical, mental, and spiritual—is fundamental to a simpler life. Finding time to stay healthy will allow you to get the most from your time and efforts.

Thoughts for Simply Living

Fear the LORD, and turn away from evil. It will be a healing for your flesh and a refreshment for your body.

PROVERBS 3:7–8 NRSV

The secret of the physical well-being of the Christian is the vitality of the divine life welling up within by virtue of his incorporation into Christ.

EVELYN FROST

"For you who revere my name, the sun of righteousness will rise with healing in its wings," says the LORD Almighty

MALACHI 4:2 NIV

Take care of your health, that it may serve you to serve God.

SAINT FRANCIS DE SALES

Remember...

_____God created you in his image. Just as God is triune—Father, Son, and Spirit—so you also are triune—mental, physical, and spiritual.

_____God intends for you to function well in all three aspects of your being.

_____When you honor your body, you are honoring God who created it.

_____Health and wellness are the keys to achieving all that God has purposed for your life.

Simplify...

Combine leisure activities in order to simplify your efforts.

Exercise with friends and combine fellowship with your workout.

Evaluate your current eating habits and note where changes need to be made.

Discipline yourself to go to bed at or near the same time each night.

If you haven't had a general physical exam in more than a year, make an appointment with your doctor.

Heal the spirit first and the body follows.

WILLIAM D. BARNHART

Minutes and Hours

Only eternal values can give meaning to temporal ones.
Time must be the servant of eternity.
Erwin W. Lutzer

Your work requires eight hours each day, your family takes another large chunk, and chores, social obligations, and exercise consume the rest. A seemingly endless list of people and activities has dibs on your time. It may seem at times that your life is flying by at breakneck speed. No wonder a simpler life looks so appealing.

Pause for a minute and consider what you would do if you had a couple extra hours each day to use in any way you please. Perhaps that would mean more time for yourself—time to read a book or the newspaper, pursue a hobby, or take a long, hot shower. Or you might choose to spend that time with your spouse, children, parents, or siblings. You might choose to have time to just sit and talk, share your hopes and dreams, get to know each other better. You might want to spend that time with friends, hanging out or watching a movie together. And you might want to spend that extra time with God, praying or studying the Bible.

The wonderful news is that you won't need those extra hours. All you really have to do to simplify your schedule is to take charge of the time you've already been given. Try this. Choose one day of your life and take it apart piece by piece. List the people and activities that take up your time. Make sure you include even the most commonplace tasks like shaving and putting on makeup.

Once you've made your list, decide if there are any activities you can eliminate from your schedule or combine with other activities to give you more free time to spend doing more of what you enjoy and of what has lasting value. Ask God to give you wisdom and guidance as you look over your list and attempt to simplify.

Every hour and minute of your day belong to you. Your schedule and your life are as simple or complicated as you decide.

One Final Thought

Looking closely at how you spend your time is the first step to simplifying your schedule and your life.

Thoughts for Simply Living

Teach us to count our days that we may gain a wise heart.
PSALM 90:12 NRSV

Time is a three-fold present: the present as we experience it, the past as a present memory, and the future as a present expectation.
SAINT AUGUSTINE OF HIPPO

For everything there is a season, and a time for every matter under heaven.
ECCLESIASTES 3:1 NRSV

One always has time enough if one will apply it.
JOHANN WOLFGANG VON GOETHE

Remember...

_____God has given everyone the same amount of time to use each day.

_____The minutes and hours of your life are a gift to you from God.

_____God has promised to help you make the most of your time here on earth.

_____God will honor the time you spend with him.

Simplify...

Give time wholeheartedly to your employer, but take charge of your personal life.

Say no to activities that consume your time but bring nothing to your life.

Schedule time for the important people and activities you have in your life.

Keep an ongoing list of ideas and insight that can help you simplify your schedule.

Spend extra time with God in prayer or Bible study.

Time is what we want most, but what alas! We use worst.

WILLIAM PENN

Getting There

A great many people go through life in bondage to success. I do not have to succeed. I have only to be true to the highest I know—success or failure are in the hands of God.

E. Stanley Jones

Success means different things to different people. Success could mean fame, wealth, achievement, or something else entirely. The Bible defines success as the fulfillment of God's purposes. In your pursuit of a simpler approach to life, ask how many of your current activities, and how much of your time, energy, and inner resources, are directed at reaching some superficial and illusive notion of success.

Are you are putting in long hours at the office, thinking that your dedication will move you up the corporate ladder? Are you depleting your finances to accumulate the trappings of success —cars, houses, clothes? Are you trying to meet someone else's expectations because you believe that success means the approval of others?

All those things complicate your life and rob you of the joy and satisfaction God intended. The answer is to use new criteria for judging success. Are you making a difference in your world? Do you have an ongoing sense of satisfaction and fulfillment?

Are you investing your life in something that has eternal value?

The Bible says that Jesus owned nothing but the clothes on his back. His life was completely devoted to doing his father's will, and his was the most significant, the most successful life ever lived. It not only changed the world but also altered the eternal relationship between God and his people.

The apostle Paul spent his later years in a prison cell and was finally martyred for his faith. Some might argue that his life didn't amount to much because he wasn't "successful." But his life continues to point people to God two thousand years after his death.

Reformulate your concept of success as you seek to find a simpler way of living. Focus your efforts on pleasing God, and you will find that it is no longer necessary to pursue the praise, expectations, and approval of others. A once frustrating quest will become a single-minded exercise in obedience.

One Final Thought

Simplifying your life includes abandoning many of the superficial trappings of success and determining to pursue the type of success that pleases God.

Thoughts for Simply Living

The plans of the diligent lead surely to abundance.

PROVERBS 21:5 NRSV

It is not your business to succeed, but to do right: when you have done so, the rest lies with God.

C. S. LEWIS

May [God] give you the desire of your heart and make all your plans succeed.

PSALM 20:4 NIV

God has not called me to be successful; he has called me to be faithful.

MOTHER TERESA

Remember...

_____True success means
pleasing only one person—God.

_____True success means
fulfilling the purpose for which
you were created.

_____Superficial success enslaves
you, but true success sets you
free to live a simple life of faith.

_____The success that God calls
you to pursue has eternal value.

Simplify...

Ask someone you consider
successful if he or she would change
anything about his or her approach
to success.

Recall which of your
personal successes gave
you the greatest sense of
satisfaction.

List the activities you take part in
during a typical week and consider
what those activities say about your
approach to success.

Add at least one activity
you feel will put you on the
road to true success.

Ask God which of your current
activities could be dropped from your
schedule in order to simplify your life.

_Risks must be taken, because the greatest hazard
in life is to risk nothing._

AUTHOR UNKNOWN

Simple Living
Simple Kindness

Kindness is the golden chain by which society is bound together.

JOHANN WOLFGANG VON GOETHE

I will tell of the kindnesses of the LORD, the deeds for which he is to be praised, according to all the LORD has done for us.
ISAIAH 63:7 NIV

As God's chosen ones, holy and beloved, clothe yourselves with compassion, kindness, humility, meekness, and patience.
COLOSSIANS 3:12 NRSV

The fruit of the Spirit is love, joy, peace, patience, kindness, generosity, faithfulness, gentleness, and self-control.
GALATIANS 5:22–23 NRSV

Have you had a kindness shown?
Pass it on;
'Twas not given for thee alone,
Pass it on;
Let it travel down the years,
Let it wipe another's tears,
'Till in Heaven the deed appears—
Pass it on.

HENRY BURTON

Working Smart

Our greatest weariness comes from work not done.
Eric Hoffer

Jobs around the house such as cooking, yard work, laundry, washing the car, and running errands have to be done. Those items probably account for the largest part of your busy day. Finding ways to master the chores before they master you is a challenge to a simpler lifestyle. The opportunities to master them are there if you know where to look.

Dedicate some time to listing the chores that need to be done in a typical week. Then put the chores into categories—yard related, car related, laundry related, meals related, and so on. Now you're better able to see how to work smarter.

Begin by finding chores you can combine. This might mean lumping together errands that are in close proximity to one another. Is the dry cleaner on the way to the hairdresser? Are there errands you can take care of on your lunch hour because they are close to the office? Rather than making a separate trip for each item, consciously work out the most effective use of your road time.

Better planning and scheduling of chores can mean more time with God—time that results in a stronger, more centered you, better able to discard superficialities and identity simple values. Controlling your chores rather than letting them control you can free your schedule for activities and relationships that further encourage you in your pursuit of a simple life. Perhaps controlling your chores will provide opportunities for you to think through situations and find solutions in other areas of your life. Controlling your chores could mean more time with your friends and family, building simple and lasting memories. And controlling your chores could also mean more time with God—time that results in a stronger, more centered you.

So embrace tips on managing chores as a way to speed you on your journey to a simpler life. Little things mean a lot.

One Final Thought

Managing chores can free up time to develop ways
to make your life simpler.

Thoughts for Simply Living

Whatever your task, put yourselves into it, as done for the Lord.

COLOSSIANS 3:23 NRSV

Lord, turn the routines of work into celebrations of love.

AUTHOR UNKNOWN

Establish the work of our hands for us—yes, establish the work of our hands.

PSALM 90:17 NIV

Manual labor to my father was not only good and decent for its own sake, but as he was given to saying, it straightened out one's thoughts.

MARY ELLEN CHASE

Remember...

_____You should be the master of your chores rather than allow your chores to master you.

_____No task is too mundane to ask for God's help in completing.

_____God can speak to your heart in the midst of thankless, mundane chores.

_____Organization can help you master your chores.

Simplify...

Create a list of chores and let family members choose which they will be responsible for each week.

Find more efficient ways to do your chores.

Make a list of chores that can be hired out—mowing the lawn or cleaning the pool, for example—and once a month pay someone else to do them for you.

Each time you begin a chore, ask God to bless your time and your effort.

Find ways to save yourself work, like hanging up clothes fresh out of the dryer or keeping a trash bag handy in the car.

Honor lies in honest toil.

GROVER CLEVELAND

Baggage

In Christ we can move out of our past into a meaningful
present and a breathtaking future.
  Erwin W. Lutzer

Have you ever tried to carry too many things at once and
found yourself losing your grip? That's what can happen when
you try to carry the baggage of your past around with you. It
unnecessarily weighs you down until your life and your busy
schedule begin to slip through your fingers. Consider this: you
can put down that baggage and walk away. The choice is yours.

Leaving the negative elements of your past behind requires
understanding and resolve. The baggage you're carrying may be
the result of your own misjudgments. Even though it's not
possible to undo mistakes you've made, you can refuse to let
them control you. Face your past mistakes honesty, learn from
them, ask God to forgive you, forgive yourself, and move on.
As you do so, God will help you walk confidently in the
present and hopefully into the future.

The baggage you are carrying from your past is the result of
the actions of other people. You can't control what others do,
but you can choose how you react. When you choose to forgive

and forget, you shift that baggage to God's hands and leave it there. Your life will immediately feel lighter and simpler.

Consider the apostle Paul who persecuted the early Christians—so much so that some were even put to death. When Paul became a believer himself, he deeply regretted his actions. Paul always acknowledged his crimes against God and man, and yet he chose not to let his past weigh him down. Instead, he handed the baggage of his past over to God and pressed forward to do all he could for the cause of Christ. In addition to his work establishing churches, he is credited with writing almost two-thirds of the New Testament—now that's a busy schedule.

God has a wonderful plan for your life, just like he did for Paul. He wants you to be free to pursue it with all your heart and soul. So while you're simplifying, looking for ways to cut back, begin by unloading the cumbersome bundles you've been carrying. Free yourself from the past and find renewed strength and stamina.

One Final Thought

You can lighten the load you are carrying in your life by leaving the baggage of your past in God's hands.

Thoughts for Simply Living

I forget what is behind me. I push hard toward what is ahead of me. I move on toward the goal to win the prize. God has appointed me to win it.

PHILIPPIANS 3:13–14 NIrV

The person who succeeds is not the one who holds back, fearing failure, nor the one who never fails . . . but rather the one who moves on in spite of failure.

CHARLES R. SWINDOLL

As far as the east is from the west, so far has he removed our transgressions from us.

PSALMS 103:12 NIV

What's gone and what's past help should be past grief.

WILLIAM SHAKESPEARE

Remember...

_____God wants you to give him your past so that you can walk unencumbered into the future he has planned for you.

_____God has assigned your past to eternal forgetfulness and wants you to do the same.

_____The future can only be chained to the past if you let it.

_____You can't change your past, but you can keep it from affecting your future.

Simplify...

Make a mental checklist of past mistakes so you'll know what baggage you may be carrying, and then list what you learned from them.

Ask God to help you deal with baggage that resurfaces in the present.

Write out Philippians 3:13–14 on an index card and put it where you will see it often as a reminder to move beyond the past and press on.

Unload the baggage you carry from your past and walk away.

Make sure your opinions that guide your life are based on facts rather than on your past perceptions.

Modern Americans travel light, with little philosophic baggage other than a fervent belief in their right to the pursuit of happiness.

GEORGE WILL

A Heart of Thankfulness

In ordinary life we hardly realize that we receive a great deal more than we give, and that it is only with gratitude that life becomes rich.
Dietrich Bonhoeffer

Have you ever wondered why God says it's so important to be grateful for what you have? One of the reasons is that a grateful heart can help you better appreciate the simple joys and blessings in life.

A grateful heart helps you to see how rich you are in the things that matter, freeing you from the endless politics of acquisition and status. A grateful heart keeps you from chasing after the illusion of success and teaches you to be content in the plan God has for you. And a grateful heart is a good receiver for the inner voice of God. It is content to be still and listen.

In the book of Luke, the story is told of ten lepers who came to Jesus for healing. Jesus sent them on their way saying they would be cleansed and healed as they went. This they all did—except one. That leper stopped when he realized that he had been healed and ran back to Jesus, thanking and praising him. The others received their healing, but nothing more. The leper who went back to show his gratitude went away with faith in the Son of God and the promise of more blessings to come.

Take time each day to thank God for the blessings he pours out on your life. Tell him why you're grateful and what that specific blessing has done for you. Also take time each day to say thank you to the faithful people God has placed in your life—the people who love you, inspire you, and make your life better. Thank them in person or in writing. And then practice your gratefulness on strangers. Tell the waitress how grateful you are for her good service, or the mechanic how grateful you are for a car that runs well.

No matter how busy you are, always take time to say thank you. Incorporate it into your lifestyle. Soon you will find that there is less time for complaining and competing and working to get ahead and more time for reaping God's simple blessings.

One Final Thought

Developing a grateful heart will help you focus on the simple blessings and joys that grace your life.

Thoughts for Simply Living

In every thing give thanks: for this is the will of God in Jesus Christ concerning you.

1 THESSALONIANS 5:18 KJV

No duty is more urgent than that of returning thanks.

SAINT AMBROSE

Offer to God a sacrifice of thanksgiving and pay your vows to the Most High.

PSALM 50:14 NRSV

To be with God wondering, that is adoration. To be with God gratefully, that is thanksgiving.

ARCHBISHOP MICHAEL RAMSAY

Remember...

_____It's easier to have gratitude when you see it as a lifestyle, not just as an occasional gesture.

_____Gratitude increases when you acknowledge that everything good originates with God.

_____The more thankful you are, the more apparent God's blessings will become in your life.

_____Being grateful through difficult times prepares you to deal with future adversity.

Simplify...

When you're saying grace before a meal, thank God for something that you've taken for granted.

Buy a friend or coworker a thank-you coffee.

Next time you're working at home, think of a simple convenience (a utensil, a tool) that makes your life easier.

Create an ongoing list of things you are grateful for.

When an elderly person reminisces about the good old days, ask her what she is most grateful for.

When eating fruit, think of the person who planted the tree.

VIETNAMESE PROVERB

Make It Fun

'Tis an ill cook that cannot lick his own fingers.
William Shakespeare

Cooking is more than a household chore. It can be an elevating experience, an opportunity to learn, even a way to express creativity, love, and hospitality. To some it can be a hobby, and to others, an obligation. In the course of your busy day, cooking may be a hassle you would just as soon skip. Or maybe you've yet to discover the simple pleasures hidden within this daily chore. There are wonderful ways to fulfill your longing for simplicity in the kitchen. Consider the following.

Cooking brings you back to basics. Stop for a moment to consider all that God has packed into the food you are preparing—an apple, a sweet potato, a filet of fish, a breast of chicken. Think about the vitamins, minerals, protein, fiber, amino acids, and carbohydrates. In your hands are the nutrients needed to sustain your life, and these nutrients are packaged in simple, beautiful packages. How can you resist thanking God for such an amazing provision to fuel your body and mind? As you thank God, your spirit will be fueled as well.

Cooking helps you to understand that God has provided much beauty and pleasure in this world for your enjoyment—bright oranges, deep yellows, delightfully unique flavors and smells. While you're cooking, it seems that the wonder of God's creative genius has settled in your very presence. As you meditate on the inventiveness of your Creator, life's challenges seem to float away.

Cooking also provides an opportunity for you to exercise creativity—an activity that reminds you once again that you are created in God's image. No matter how many times you've prepared a particular dish, you can always find a way to add something new.

You may find it easier to swing through the drive-through window at the nearest fast-food restaurant. But when you consider how much creating even one home cooked meal a week can bring to your life in terms of thankfulness, satisfaction, creative expression, and blessing to yourself and others, you may decide that it's time to get back to basics in the kitchen.

One Final Thought

Cooking, by its very nature, is an activity that can help you connect with God, with others, and with the world around you.

Thoughts for Simply Living

The manna was like coriander seed and looked like resin.
The people went around gathering it, and then ground it in
a handmill or crushed it in a mortar. They cooked it in a pot
or made it into cakes.

NUMBERS 11:7 NIV

The food you prepare for your body also nourishes your soul.

JEFFREY WASHINGTON

Bring hither the fatted calf and kill it; and let us eat
and be merry.

LUKE 15:23 KJV

The wonderful aroma of fresh-baked bread, the warm, steamy goodness of
home-made soup, the rich, simple pleasure of icing a cake—these are
the joys of cooking.

ERNEST HARVEY

Remember...

_____Cooking offers a daily forum for creativity.

_____God not only created your body to need food, he gave you the gift of enjoying the preparation of food as well.

_____God has created a generous variety of foods for you to prepare.

_____Cooking for someone is one of the most practical ways you can show God's love.

Simplify...

Next time you're preparing dinner, double the recipe and take the extra to a busy friend.

Try a new recipe each week.

When you're invited for dinner at the home of a good cook, ask if you can come early and learn some new cooking techniques.

Invite your family members to cook with you.

Use the money you would spend on a birthday gift for a friend or family member to prepare a special dinner for that person.

I was 32 when I started cooking; up until then, I just ate.

JULIA CHILD

New Ways

Change is not something without inconvenience, even from worse to better.
Richard Hooker

Your decision to simplify your life will mean tampering with your comfort zone. It will mean stepping out in faith to embrace new insights and ways of doing things. It will mean relaxing your grip on the old and letting God help you discover the new. It will mean accepting challenges in every area of your life. In a word, it will mean change. Change isn't always easy, but when God's hand is in it, it is always beneficial.

The Bible says that the disciples of Jesus embraced great change in their lives in order to follow him. The fishermen left their nets, the physician left his patients, the tax collector left his coveted government job. They stepped away from their busy schedules and out of their comfort zones in order to follow Jesus to a better life—a life that exchanged earthly joys for heavenly ones.

After the resurrection of Christ, the early Christians were also forced to make great changes in their perspectives and

lifestyles. Although they came from diverse social groups and professions, they came together as sisters and brothers in the faith, equal before God. Many among them had been wealthy and even more had been poor, but the Bible says that they shared all things in common. They traded the social and economic norms they had known for simple lives of faith.

The simpler life you seek begins and ends with change. Perhaps adopting a simpler life would mean leaving your comfortable job behind to follow God's calling. It could mean trading in a large and costly home for a smaller, more manageable, more economical one. It could mean learning to tend a garden or attending a different church. Whatever it is, you can do it. You can afford to risk change for the same reason the New Testament Christians did—God is your anchor. He is unchanging and holds you steady as you step resolutely out of your comfort zone

One Final Thought

Change is fundamental to facilitating the simpler life you desire.

Thoughts for Simply Living

Jesus said, "I tell you the truth, unless you change and become like little children, you will never enter the kingdom of heaven."

MATTHEW 18:3 NIV

We can change, slowly and steadily, if we set our will to it.

ROBERT HUGH BENSON

Be made new in the attitude of your minds.

EPHESIANS 4:23 NIV

In a higher world it is otherwise, but here below to live is to change, and to be perfect is to have changed often.

JOHN HENRY NEWMAN

Remember...

_____God uses change to give you new insights and possibilities to bring you closer to him.

_____Even positive changes carry a certain level of stress with them.

_____Accepting new challenges and opportunities will allow God to use you in many new ways.

_____Accepting change is acknowledging that God has something better in store for you.

Simplify...

Identify three changes that you feel God is urging you to make in your life.

Ask your doctor what changes you need to make to your lifestyle in order to lead a healthier life.

Pray that God will identify one area of your work life where change could help you release stress and do a better job.

Think of a specific area where you have resisted change and determine to pray about it.

Ask yourself what change you could make in your schedule that will provide you with more time to spend with God.

Change is a challenge and an opportunity, not a threat.

PRINCE PHILLIP OF ENGLAND

Simple Living
Simple Wisdom

Men may acquire knowledge, but wisdom is a gift direct from God.

BOB JONES

The testimony of the LORD is sure, making wise the simple.

PSALM 19:7 KJV

The fear of the LORD is the beginning of wisdom.

PSALM 111:10 KJV

The wisdom from above is first pure, then peaceable, gentle, willing to yield; full of mercy and good fruits, without a trace of partiality or hypocrisy.

JAMES 3:17 NRSV

True wisdom is in leaning
On Jesus Christ, our Lord;
True wisdom is in trusting
His own life-giving Word;
True wisdom is in living
Near Jesus every day;
True wisdom is in walking
Where He shall lead the way.

AUTHOR UNKNOWN

The Truth About Work

Jesus knows we must come apart and rest awhile,
or else we may just plain come apart.
> Vance Havner

Rest is as important to the work process as initiative and drive. Rest directly enhances productivity and fulfillment and has a way of simplifying your day-to-day challenges by increasing your stamina and making it easier for you to find and facilitate solutions.

In athletic competition, at the most crucial point in the game, coaches will often rest their star players for a brief time, giving them the extra edge to push on to the finish. In the most practical aspects of your day-to-day life, resting gives you the chance to unclutter your thoughts, replenish your physical strength, shore up your immune system, and gain strength.

Even the greatest sports heroes of all time rarely played full games. Their victories were always a combination of hard work and strategic rests or time-outs. God himself rested, and in so doing prepared a model for you to do the same in your life.

When deadlines are bearing down on you, when the week seems a few days too short, it's tempting to feel guilty about taking a break. But taking a significant rest to recharge your batteries may be the most productive avenue you can take on your way to achieving the goals set before you.

In broader terms, rest puts things into perspective by allowing you to take a step back from a situation. It gives God a chance to speak to you. It gives him an opportunity to lift your thoughts above the busyness of life to focus for a time on the spiritual aspects of your life.

You can find freedom in that respite by acknowledging that God created rest and that it is an important component in your busy life. With rest, you'll keep yourself fresh, be able to use your mental abilities to their fullest, and find the emotional and physical stamina needed to achieve your daily aspirations. When you are functioning at your peak, every part of your life will seem much simpler.

One Final Thought

Taking time for rest helps you simplify by increasing your stamina, stimulating your creativity, and helping you focus.

Thoughts for Simply Living

Be still, and know that I am God.

PSALM 46:10 KJV

Jesus can expound nothing until we get through all the noisy questions of the head and are alone with him.

OSWALD CHAMBERS

Those who trust in the LORD will receive new strength. They will fly as high as eagles. They will run and not get tired. They will walk and not grow weak.

ISAIAH 40:31 NIrV

Some seek bread; and some seek wealth and ease; and some seek fame, but all are seeking rest.

FREDERICK LANGBRIDGE

Remember...

_____Rest renews and restores your body, soul, and spirit.

_____Spiritual rest comes from spending time with God.

_____Rest gives you an opportunity to remove the static from your busy mind and focus on the voice of God.

_____God made rest an important element following the work of creation by resting on the seventh day as an example for us.

Simplify...

Schedule regular rest periods in your week.

Use the minutes you wait for other people to meditate on a Scripture verse.

Take an occasional one-hour media break from radio, TV, telephone, and your computer.

When you're stuck in traffic, turn the radio to a station that plays classical or worship music.

Surprise your spouse or a friend by taking a Friday afternoon off and spending it with him or her.

There is no music in a "rest" but there is the making of music in it.

JOHN RUSKIN

What's Ahead

The next moment is as much beyond our grasp and as much in God's care as that a hundred years away.

C. S. Lewis

The future is a strange and mysterious unknown always waiting just ahead. You may be able to influence the future with good planning and wise choices, but the future has a way of confounding even the best planners. Trying to prepare for all situations that the future may drop in your path can be complex and exhausting. Simplicity in your approach to the future comes by trusting God, holding tightly to God's hand, and listening to his voice inside your heart.

God has a great and wonderful plan for your life, and he is committed to helping you find and fulfill that plan. He sees clearly the things that you cannot. With his guidance, you can meet any challenge the future might hold for you.

Throughout history, men and women have tried to know and understand coming events, but the Bible says God is the only true reference for what lies ahead. Trusting in any other system may leave you with more questions than answers. Trusting God will always keep you safe and satisfied.

God has set in place a secure system for learning everything you need to know in order to successfully fulfill your future destiny. He has given you the Bible filled with information about future events and eternal principles. This includes an understanding that this earthly life is only a part of what God has in store for you. You can know that God will be with you no matter what you may have to face in this life.

Place your future in God's hands. Rejoice in the security of knowing he will be walking at your side throughout your earthly life and even in the eternity to come. Whatever comes your way, the two of you can face it and conquer it together.

One Final Thought

God knows everything that the future holds for you, and he is walking at your side every step of the way.

Thoughts for Simply Living

There is surely a future hope for you, and your hope will not be cut off.

> PROVERBS 23:18 NIV

Commit your work to the LORD, and your plans will be established.

> PROVERBS 16:3 NRSV

In his heart a man plans his course, but the LORD determines his steps.

> PROVERBS 16:9 NIV

Because eternity was closeted in time, He is my open door to forever.

> LUCI SHAW

Remember...

_____God is committed to your success in the future.

_____God has placed the answers to many of your questions in the Bible.

_____You can influence the future, but only God can control it.

_____Your future is as bright as the promises of God.

Simplify...

When you are tempted to waste time being anxious about the future, remember all the difficult times in the past that God brought you through.

Identify what you can plan for and what you can't plan for.

Start a list of life goals, including both grand and small desires.

Pray that God will prepare you for the plans he has for you.

Speak positively about the future, verbalizing your confidence in God as the one who will lead the way for you.

My interest is in the future, because I'm going to spend the rest of my life there.

CHARLES KETTERING

Growing in Understanding

It is possible to store the mind with a million facts and still be entirely uneducated.

Alec Bourne

Learning is a lifelong process. It doesn't end the day you donned a flowing robe and tasseled cap and grasped a diploma. You will have many more opportunities to learn new ways of doing things as you pursue your desire to simplify your life. Learning new ways may seem more practical than spiritual, but God is in it.

Learning new strategies for reaching new markets, creating new products for a new generation, and developing ways to enhance relationships with colleagues present opportunities for continued learning. Keeping up to date on health issues can help you stay healthy and avoid the complications and lost time that illness entails. Keeping current with nutritional guidelines will help you tailor your eating to your body's needs.

A simpler diet might mean that you have to learn the benefits of organically grown food, for instance. A simpler work environment might require that you learn new technologies. A simpler spiritual life may mean that you'll need to reassess your God-given talents and gifts. Learning how to better manage your finances can help you do more with less, lessening stress and giving you more control over debt and possessions.

Learning new ways to deal with people can help you simplify your relationships with coworkers, family members, friends, and neighbors. Learning more about God can make your life simpler by helping you identify and change patterns in your life that have been holding you back from becoming all he intended you to be. Learning the principles God has placed in the Bible—principles concerning money, attitudes, character, and relationships, for example—can help you avoid missteps and complications.

The Bible doesn't encourage you to walk through life ignorantly accepting what you hear. God knows that the more you know, the more his place in your life will be confirmed rather than negated. So don't hold back. Learn all you can and then put it into practice.

One Final Thought

Learning can help you simplify your life by providing you with new ways of doing things.

Thoughts for Simply Living

Let the wise listen and add to their learning.

PROVERBS 1:5 NIV

In a time of drastic change, it is the learners who inherit the future.

ERIC HOFFER

If any of you is lacking in wisdom, ask God,
who gives to all generously and ungrudgingly,
and it will be given you.

JAMES 1:5 NRSV

God alone, through his Word, instructs the heart.

MARTIN LUTHER

Remember...

_____God has been called the "great teacher." He wants you to be as knowledgeable as possible.

_____The principles taught in the Bible are often practical, everyday truths that can help you live a less stressful, more productive life.

_____God is interested in constant learning in every area of your being—body, mind, and spirit.

_____The Holy Spirit has been sent to help you learn more and more about the person and character of God.

Simplify...

Make an effort to learn from the life experience of others—especially in terms of assessing priorities for your busy life.

Learn all you can about how to organize and balance your schedule.

Make a list of topics you need to learn more about in order to simplify your life.

Keep a small notebook to jot down simplification tips you've learned.

Look for a person who has succeeded in simplifying his or her life and learn how he or she did it.

We often learn great lessons in simple everyday ways.

PEARL BUCK

Playing Right

Life lived amidst tension and busyness needs leisure.
Leisure that re-creates and renews.
> Neil C. Strait

A time of respite is important to your well-being. It can be a time to gain perspective, grow closer to God, spend time with your family, and bring renewal to your body, soul, and spirit. In order to gain that kind of benefit, it's important to avoid trips that leave you running frantically from one activity to another. Simplify your vacation and you will find another key to simplifying your life.

The Bible says that Jesus often took time alone to reconnect with God and renew his strength. That time he spent alone with God was a vacation for his body and soul. Make sure your vacation includes time alone with God, time to feel his love and hear his voice speaking to your heart.

Choose a vacation plan that will also have opportunities to communicate with your family members. Plan activities that allow your loved ones to focus on each other— lounging on the beach together, sauntering down quiet paths on the backs of horses, or sitting on the shore with your fishing poles.

When planning your vacation, allow for time to reflect on your life and what you feel is important to you. Answer the questions you've been asking yourself—those questions that your busy schedule hasn't allowed you to deal with.

Overplanning can leave you feeling like you're still running to get everything done. It's important to leave much of your vacation time open ended so that you can take advantage of unexpected opportunities to rest and renew yourself. Eat when you feel hungry, sleep when you feel sleepy. During your special vacation time, take things as they come.

Wherever you choose to vacation, make it a time for enjoying the simple pleasures of life, a time for celebrating the goodness of God, a time for slowing down and giving God a chance to restore your enthusiasm for living. When vacation serves the purpose for which it was intended, life after vacation will seem much simpler.

One Final Thought

Taking a vacation is a great way to slow you down and gain perspective on your hectic life.

Thoughts for Simply Living

Jesus said to them, "Come away to a deserted place all by
yourselves and rest a while."

MARK 6:31 NRSV

Travel to the far corners of the earth and you'll still see God at work in you.

SANFORD CARLETON

Jesus often withdrew to lonely places and prayed.

LUKE 5:16 NIV

Leisure wisely taken is a God-given reward for hard work and
a blessed respite for the soul.

ANDREA GARNEY

Remember...

_____By example, Jesus instructs us to take a break from busyness to rest and be renewed.

_____Taking a break can add perspective and renewed vision to your day-to-day life.

_____Vacations provide opportunities for reflection and reconnection with God.

_____God designed rest to enrich your life, so enjoy it without feeling guilty.

Simplify...

Schedule "unscheduled" periods throughout your vacation simply for relaxation and personal reflection.

Set a specific budget for your vacation and stick with it. Debt creates stress and stress complicates your life.

Before you start planning, ask yourself about the specific purpose of your vacation.

Read a short travel guide or magazine article about a place you would like to visit.

Give yourself time to spend with God on your next vacation.

When play is at its best, something of the presence of God breaks into our lives and redemptive powers are experienced.

PETER BERGER

A Few Simple Rules

Remember the Lord your God, for it is he who gives you the ability
to produce wealth.
Deuteronomy 8:17 NIV

One encompassing financial principle comes before all
money-management tips: all resources come from God.
Your money is really his. He believes in you enough to put
you in charge of a small part of his kingdom. When you see
your resources as part of God's greater plan, the motivation
to spend wisely and give freely is built right in, which
simplifies your decisions about the way you manage your
money.

Observing a few guidelines can help you make wiser
decisions about the resources God has entrusted you with.
Try these suggestions.

Acknowledge God as the source of all your finances—
whether they be great or small—by setting aside a
percentage of your income to tithe to your church or give to
a worthy cause or someone in need in God's name.

Set a realistic budget that includes plans for the future.
Instead of viewing a surplus (such as a tax refund) as an

invitation to buy a new golf bag, get in the habit of seeing that extra cash as a chance to contribute to a contingency fund (such as for car maintenance, household emergencies, or educational needs), a retirement account, or to help out someone who needs a hand that month.

Wait until you have the money before you make a purchase. Credit cards are a great way to manage your monthly expenditures only if you are in the habit of paying them off in full every month. If you see an extra item, make a plan to put aside a small amount of your surplus each pay period.

When paying off your debts, aggressively pay off the smallest ones first. You'll get a sense of accomplishment from getting those out of the way early.

You are a busy person—too busy to spend time working through each financial decision. It simplifies things greatly to acknowledge God as your source and set policies ahead of time to govern your financial management.

One Final Thought

You can make managing your finances much easier by acknowledging God as your source and observing good financial guidelines.

Thoughts for Simply Living

The blessing of the LORD brings wealth, and he adds no trouble to it.

PROVERBS 10:22 NIV

If a person gets his attitude toward money straight, it will help straighten out almost every other area in his life.

BILLY GRAHAM

He who gathers money little by little makes it grow.

PROVERBS 13:11 NIV

If a man's religion does not affect his use of money, that man's religion is vain.

HUGH MARTIN

Remember...

_____God wouldn't entrust you with his resources without giving you access to the tools to manage them.

_____Giving back to God is both an act of faith and an act of worship.

_____Firm financial footing involves planning for the future now.

_____True prosperity comes when you make God your first priority and allow him to play an active role in your financial planning.

Simplify...

Open a contingency account and deposit a monthly sum (even if it's only a modest amount) into that fund.

Establish a general budget to help you track your spending.

Agree with family members on a certain percentage (10 percent or more) to give back to God each month.

Contribute to your savings account and your retirement fund every month.

Begin to wean yourself off of credit cards by discontinuing all but the two with the lowest interest rates and broadest use.

If you want to make your money go as far as possible, give it to foreign missions.

AUTHOR UNKNOWN

Simple Living
Simple Righteousness

My hope is built on nothing less than Jesus' blood and righteousness.

EDMUND MORE

The effect of righteousness will be peace, and the result of righteousness, quietness and trust forever.
ISAIAH 32:17 NRSV

Jesus said, "Blessed are those who hunger and thirst for righteousness, for they will be filled."
MATTHEW 5:6 NRSV

You bless the righteous, O LORD; you cover them with favor as with a shield.
PSALM 5:12 NRSV

The man of life upright,
Whose guiltless heart is free
From all dishonest deeds
Or thought of vanity.

Good thoughts his only friends,
His wealth a well-spent age,
The earth his sober inn
And quiet pilgrimage.

THOMAS CAMPION

Real Living

The vigor of our spiritual life will be in exact proportion to the place held by the Bible in our life and thoughts.

George Müller

Within the pages of the Bible, you will find the story of God's interactions with mankind—his thoughts, his plans, his intentions, and his wisdom for those he created in his very own image. No wonder it is the perfect guide for daily living. In your pursuit of a simpler life, the Bible should be the first place you go to gain perspective and inspiration. Finding time in your busy schedule to read just a little each day will help you get on track with your goal and stay there.

You might want to begin with the book of Proverbs, which is dedicated to advice that will help you gain wisdom and understanding about life's dealings. You will find timeless principles such as "When pride comes, then comes disgrace, but with humility comes wisdom" (Proverbs 11:2). Being prideful will complicate your life, while humility will help you stay balanced, avoiding much of the clutter and dead ends that come from chasing after ego.

The book of Ecclesiastes tells the reader that only eternal

values matter. After reviewing the scope of man's activities, Ecclesiastes 12:13 states the author's conclusions: "Now all has been heard; here is the conclusion of the matter: Fear God and keep his commandments, for this is the whole duty of man." Knowing what really matters will help you understand how to make changes while preserving the essentials.

In the New Testament, the lives of Jesus and his disciples provide an example of simple living. With few if any possessions of their own, they dedicated themselves to pursuing the destiny God had placed before them. The early Christians surrendered their right to private property and lived with all things in common. They were subjugating the importance of earthly possessions in favor of heavenly treasure.

Go to the Bible's pages often as you seek to establish a life that gets back to basics and lends itself to the important values of life. As you read, you will begin to see how to live a wiser, simpler lifestyle—and that is likely to be just the beginning of what you will learn from the Book of all books.

One Final Thought

The Bible provides wisdom and understanding for living a simple life.

Thoughts for Simply Living

All Scripture is God-breathed and is useful for teaching, rebuking, correcting and training in righteousness, so that the man of God may be thoroughly equipped for every good work.

> 2 Timothy 3:16–17 NIV

The Bible is a book of faith, and a book of doctrine, and a book of morals, and a book of religion, of especial revelation from God.

> DANIEL WEBSTER

All human beings are like grass, and all their glory is like wild flowers. The grass withers, and the flowers fall, but the word of the Lord remains forever.

> 1 PETER 1:24–25 NIV

The books of men have their day and grow obsolete. God's Word is like Himself, "the same yesterday, today, and forever."

> ROBERT PAYNE SMITH

Remember...

_____God has given you the Bible as a guide to help you deal with the issues of life.

_____God's Spirit inspired the writers of the Bible.

_____The principles put forth in the Bible continue to stand the test of time.

_____The Bible contains the foundation stones for building a meaningful and purposeful life.

Simplify...

Read wise insights from Proverbs, Ecclesiastes, Matthew, Mark, Luke, John, or Acts.

Share the principles you've learned with others.

Jot down principles for simple living that you find as you read through these books.

Pray over the principles you are finding and ask God which ones are most needed in your life.

Each month, deliberately begin to assimilate one of these principles into your daily living.

B.I.B.L.E: Basic Instruction Before Leaving Earth.

Author Unknown

Looking Back

O God . . . on my bed I remember you;
I think of you through the watches of the night.
Psalm 53:1, 6 NIV

Memories can play an important role in your quest for a simple life—your memories and the memories of others provide experiential understanding and insight that can help you decide what pursuits you can eliminate or reduce and what must be preserved and cherished.

The wonderful thing about memories is that they crystallize an action or conversation down to its simplest form. If you look back, you'll probably be able to remember best those things that are most important. Reflect for a moment on your childhood and focus on some of the primary memories that come to your mind. They might be sharing an ice-cream cone with your father or walking with your mother on your first day of school. Perhaps it's a memory that involves a grandparent or sibling.

What you probably remember most clearly about sharing that ice-cream cone with your father is not the flavor of the ice cream, but the warm and happy feeling of being with your dad. One of the reasons for simplifying your life is to make room for enjoying the company of those you love. Your memories help you identify those things that have lasting value.

Memories can help you sift through the clutter of life and find the essentials. For example, some of the struggles your parents had might help you make better decisions about what's important as you pursue your career and out-of-home activities.

Your memories of your relationship with God are more important than any other memories you might have. Think about the times that you have really felt close to God. Meditate on those times. Let them inspire you to continue to draw near to him—each day, each hour. When you do, you will remember how simple life becomes in the light of his presence.

Let your memories help you as you seek a simpler life.

One Final Thought

Memories can help you reach your goal of a simpler life by reminding you of those things in your life that have eternal value.

Thoughts for Simply Living

Jesus said, "The Helper, the Holy Spirit, whom the Father will send in my name, will teach you everything and make you remember all that I have told you."

JOHN 14:26 GNT

Memory tempers prosperity, mitigates adversity, controls youth, and delights old age.

AUTHOR UNKNOWN

God also said to Moses, "Say to the Israelites, 'The LORD, the God of your fathers . . . has sent me to you. This is my name forever, the name by which I am to be remembered from generation to generation.' "

EXODUS 3:15 NIV

Memory is the cabinet of imagination, the treasury of reason, the registry of conscience, and the council chamber of thought.

SAINT BASIL

Remember...

_____Your memory is a God-given gift.

_____The Bible says that if you live righteously, your memory will be blessed.

_____Your memory can help you better navigate the present and the future.

_____If you remember where you came from, you can better understand how to get where you want to go.

Simplify...

Spend some time conversing with an older relative and mining his or her memories to identify principles of enduring value.

Pass on to your younger family members your most precious memories.

Think about good memories you have of growing up and what insights you can draw from them to order your present life.

Meditate on the special times you've had with God in prayer or Bible reading.

Ask a Christian friend to recall a few of his or her most important encounters with God; listen for important principles.

You can go back and have what you like if you remember it well enough.

RICHARD LLEWELLYN

Inner Quiet

Solitude is essentially the discovery and acceptance of our uniqueness.
Lawrence Freeman

Your quest to find a simpler life will be more quickly realized when you learn to appreciate solitude—time alone to sort through your thoughts and feelings. Solitude affords an opportunity to escape the busyness all around you and allow your heart to respond to the still, small voice of God. Invite him to share your solitude and you will experience a few moments of life in its simplest form—unimportant details will fall from sight and clarity of thought and mind will replace confusion and fear.

In the rush of your busy life, finding time for solitude may seem like an impossible dream. The answer is to determine to make room for it, just as Jesus did.

Jesus was a busy man. He often ministered to crowds of people from dawn to dusk and then spent time teaching his disciples. He knew that his ministry would be short, and he was eager to accomplish all that God had sent him to do. Still, in the midst of all the demands on his time, the Bible says he found opportunities to slip away by himself and spend time alone with God. During those periods of solitude, he probably shook off the nonessentials and focused on his mission. By finding time for solitude, he gained the renewed strength and clarity he needed to return to his task.

When your mind begins to feel overwhelmed, solitude will work for you, just as it did for Jesus. Like a closet filled to overflowing, you need time apart to sort through and unload those thoughts and images that distract you. You need time to reconnect with God and focus again on the simple, basic principles he has called you to live by.

Jesus knew that solitude—time apart with God—was the provision he had been given in order to keep his life and calling simple and unpolluted by the world. Solitude will help you, too. Use it to help you stay grounded in the purposes God has established for your life.

One Final Thought

Solitude is time spent alone blocking out the busy details of life and listening to God's voice

Thoughts for Simply Living

In the morning, rising up a great while before day, [Jesus]
went out, and departed into a solitary place, and there prayed.

MARK 1:35 KJV

Language has created the word loneliness to express the pain of being alone,
and the word solitude to express the glory of being alone.

PAUL TILLICH

In quietness and trust is your strength.

ISAIAH 30:15 NIV

Develop the art of solitude and you will unearth the gift of serenity.

WILLIAM ARTHUR WARD

Remember...

_____Jesus embraced solitude and set it as a practice for you to follow.

_____Solitude shuts out the voices of the world around you and allows you to listen to the voice of God.

_____Time alone with God helps you to stay focused on the basics and to shake off the things that have no lasting value.

_____Solitude is a gift from God and a tool he urges you to use in your quest to simplify your life.

Simplify...

Schedule a regular time each day to be alone with God.

Learn to recognize your limits; catch a few minutes alone before you reach overload.

Choose a particular place at home or at work where you can be alone.

Explain to your family or close friends your need for alone time.

Use your alone time to let God weed out your busy thoughts and simplify your perspective.

Aloneness is more that social detachment. It is a matter of resting the mind from the heavy work of thinking.

CALVIN MILLER

Learning from Others

The wise listen to advice.
Proverbs 12:15 NRSV

Good advice can make your life simpler by allowing you to learn through the experience of others. Think about how gratifying it would be to avoid some of the missteps, take the right path the first time, and find answers without the frustrating process of trial and error. As you seek new ways to simplify your life, one way you might want to try is taking advice from people you trust.

Many organizations offer advice and counsel to those who are looking. One of those is an organization called SCORE (Service Corps of Retired Executives), which is made up of retired executives willing to share what they've learned in the business world. Resources like this exist almost everywhere and are easy to find.

Older men and women who have raised their children are another source of great advice. Listening to what they have to say can help you make things run better at home with the kids. And of course, many older Christians would be glad to share their advice and insights with you if you desire to grow in your relationship with God. If you don't know anyone who could serve in this capacity, you might ask a local clergyman to suggest someone.

In regard to finances, you may want to seek out a professional adviser or a friend or family member who has done well financially. Or ask people who have raised large families on a limited budget for advice about how to make the most of your financial resources.

In your journey to a simpler lifestyle, it makes sense to gain all the insights you can from others. Learning everything through first-hand experience wastes resources that could be better used elsewhere. When you do find good advice, pray about it and then put it into practice. Remember, advice is only good if you use it. Once you do, you'll begin to appreciate how many steps you can save, problems you can avoid, and time you garner for other pursuits.

One Final Thought

Seeking out good advice from others can help you simplify your life by helping you make better choices.

Thoughts for Simply Living

Plans are established by taking advice.

PROVERBS 20:18 NRSV

No gift is more precious than good advice.

DESIDERIUS ERASMUS

Plans fail for lack of counsel, but with many advisers they succeed.

PROVERBS 15:22 NIV

Write down the advice of him who loves you, though you like it not at present.

ENGLISH PROVERB

Remember...

_____Good advice is available in a variety of forms; if you're looking for it, you will find it.

_____The Bible says that those who listen to advice are wise.

_____Good advice can help you cut through barriers and grow in your relationship with God.

_____Good advice can help you get things right the first time and free up more time, energy, and resources for other pursuits.

Simplify...

Locate a mentor who can give you valuable advice on a particular aspect of your life.

> Meet with your mentor regularly and ask questions each time you're together.

Check out the advice you've been given with at least one other person to make sure it's valid.

> Pray about how you can implement this advice in ways that will simplify your life.

Make a record of the advice you will need at a later stage of your life.

I not only use all the brains I have but all I can borrow.

WOODROW WILSON

Free to Live

Let us keep our spirits unentangled by avoiding all appearance of evil, and all ways that lead there.

John Owen

Pause for a moment to consider why you are seeking to simplify your life. Is it because you are tired of running after superficialities and wish to focus on those things that have true and lasting value? Perhaps you feel your life has become tangled, complicated, and out of control. You want to free yourself to ensure that your life makes a difference. The success of your mission depends on your determination to turn your back on the temptations that can derail you and leave your life anything but simple.

Everyone is subject to temptation. The Bible says that even Jesus was tempted, and yet he stood firm and resisted. It's a fact that temptation will always be a challenge. But the Bible also says that it's a battle you can win with God's help. Victory will help you gain and maintain the simple lifestyle you're striving for.

The first step to resisting temptation is to clearly understand its danger. Temptation is often a surprise attack.

You must train yourself to be vigilant, watchful, and aware of your vulnerabilities. Your resistance is based on preparedness.

The second step is to realize that you are helpless to resist temptation without God's help. In 1 Peter 1:5, you will read that you are protected by the power of God. What a promise! When you are tempted you can turn to God and ask for his power to help you resist.

The third step is to recognize that God has given you two important tools with which to resist the temptations in your life—the Bible and prayer. Jesus urged his disciples to pray that they would not enter into temptation, and he resisted temptation by knowing and reciting the Word of God to his tempter.

Your quest for simplicity is a virtuous one. Facilitate it by staying grounded in prayer and the Word of God. It's a battle you can win.

One Final Thought

Resisting temptation can help you achieve your goal of a simpler life by keeping your life free of complications and entanglements.

Thoughts for Simply Living

Jesus prayed, "Lead us not into temptation, but deliver us from the evil one."

MATTHEW 6:13 NIV

Temptation provokes me to look upward to God.

JOHN BUNYAN

No one, when tempted, should say, "I am being tempted by God"; for God cannot be tempted by evil and he himself tempts no one.

JAMES 1:13 NRSV

There was never anyone so good that he was exempt from trials and temptations.

AUTHOR UNKNOWN

Remember...

_____Resisting temptation will help you keep your life simple and on track.

_____God has given you the power to overcome temptation.

_____Prayer and the Bible can help you overcome temptation.

_____Temptation cannot defeat you if you refuse to let it.

Simplify...

Identify which areas (money, success, relationships) make you vulnerable to temptation.

Develop strategies for resisting temptation in these areas.

Acknowledge to God that you need his help in order to successfully resist temptation in those areas.

Offer yourself to God each day and ask that he protect you from temptation.

Find verses in the Bible that will help you fight off temptation when it comes.

I cannot keep birds from flying over my head, but I can keep them from building under my hat.

MARTIN LUTHER

Simple Living
Simple Peace

Christ alone can bring lasting peace—peace with God—peace among men and nations—and peace within our hearts.

BILLY GRAHAM

Do not be anxious about anything, but in everything, by prayer and petition, with thanksgiving, present your requests to God. And the peace of God, which transcends all understanding, will guard your hearts and your minds in Christ Jesus.
PHILIPPIANS 4:6–7 NIV

Jesus said, "Peace I leave with you; my peace I give you. I do not give to you as the world gives. Do not let your hearts be troubled and do not be afraid."
JOHN 14:27 NIV

To set the mind on the Spirit is life and peace.
ROMANS 8:6 NRSV

Like a river glorious is God's perfect peace;

Over all victorious to its bright increase;

Perfect, yet it floweth fuller every day;

Perfect, yet it groweth deeper all the way.

FRANCES RIDLEY HAVERGAL

Meaningful Exchanges

Gift giving should not be a form of competition, an exercise in one-upmanship, but rather the sincere gesture of a loving heart.
Andrea Garney

Giving a gift on a special occasion is a wonderful custom—one that should be encouraged. But you can do it without going broke or being pulled into the cycle of unreasonable expectations, status issues, and guilt. Simplify your life by adopting a policy of heartfelt gift-giving.

Begin to transform your gift-giving by determining not to try to match a gift given to you in terms of size or price. The obligation to reciprocate in kind turns an act of kindness into a competition and stifles the sense of joy that should be enjoyed when giving a gift. It also makes the receiver feel obligated to meet your bid and raise it.

Review the special interests, likes, and dislikes of the person you are giving the gift to. Choose a gift that will please the recipient. The joy you feel when you present someone with a gift and see his or her face light up with happiness is a reminder of why it's important to give from the heart.

Setting spending limits is an effective way to encourage everyone—family, friends, coworkers, and yourself—to become heartfelt givers.

God gave you the ultimate heart-felt gift when he sent his son, Jesus, to pay the penalty for your sins. He gave his gift freely without thought of reciprocation, even when he knew you could never return his gift in kind. And God's greatest gift was very personal—presented to you with love and understanding of your specific needs. Wouldn't it be wise to give with the same pure motives that inspired God's greatest gift to you?

When you made your decision to simplify your life, gift-giving may have been one of the first areas you thought about. And it should be. All it takes to restore giving as a simple pleasure both for you and for the one receiving the gift is to follow God's example, and reach out with your heart.

One Final Thought

Simplify your life by choosing gifts from the heart.

Thoughts for Simply Living

Each of you must give as you have made up your mind, not reluctantly or under compulsion, for God loves a cheerful giver.

2 CORINTHIANS NRSV

Blessed are those who can give without remembering and take without forgetting.

ELIZABETH BIBESCO

The Lord Jesus himself said:
"It is more blessed to give than to receive."

ACTS 20:35 NIV

When you give, see that you give that which multiplies in giving.

RAYMOND LULL

Remember...

_____God has set the standard for heartfelt giving.

_____God gives to his children freely and from the heart.

_____God encourages you to give from a sense of love and caring.

_____God wants you to enjoy giving, just as he does.

Simplify...

Set a spending cap on individual gifts for Christmas and birthdays.

Consider doing something for someone rather than buying something.

Ask God to show you how to use the talents he's given you to create meaningful gifts.

Make a habit of praying for the recipient of the gift before you select it.

Make a decision not to respond to the tyranny of obligation giving.

The best gifts are those which expect no return.

NORWEGIAN PROVERB

A Simple Conversation

I live in the spirit of prayer. I pray as I walk about, when I lie down,
and when I rise up. And the answers are always coming.
George Miller

Prayer is the focal point of a simple life and for good
reason. Prayer is petition, thanksgiving, worship, and much
more. Prayer is communication and fellowship with the
One who matters—God, your Creator.

Imagine for a moment that you are visiting one of the
many historic convents and monasteries. These are places
where men and women have devoted their lives to God and
embraced the sparest of lifestyles. Giving up all but a few
meager possessions, they have stripped themselves of
everything that would distract them from their spiritual
focus—personal clothing, property, careers, family, and, for
some, speech. Many devote themselves instead to prayer.

You may not be called to lead such an extreme life. But
you can gain insight from the example of those who have
chosen to put all else aside to focus on prayer. Even if you
are wanting to do no more than trim back the excesses and
focus on core issues, prayer can help you achieve and

maintain the simplicity you desire. And prayer does so in many wonderful ways.

Prayer invites you to see things through the eyes of God rather than the eyes of ego. As you spend time in prayer, you will almost certainly find yourself more grounded, more centered, and more levelheaded. You may soon find that the superficialities that have impeded your joy and caused you to long for a simpler, more meaningful existence are falling away.

Prayer keeps you in tune with God's purposes for your life. Prayer provides clarity, confidence, and direction. When you are spending time praying for others, you will find it easier to practice humility, forgiveness, and caring. In addition, prayer helps you unload worry and anxiety.

As you move forward in your commitment to simple living, bolster every aspect of your being—your body, your mind, and your spirit—by making prayer a constant and familiar friend.

One Final Thought

Prayer will help you achieve and maintain a simple life.

Thoughts for Simply Living

Devote yourselves to prayer, being watchful and thankful.
COLOSSIANS 4:2 NIV

Prayer takes place in the heart, not in the head.
CARLO CARRETTO

Pray in the Spirit on all occasions with all kinds of prayers and requests.
EPHESIANS 6:18 NIV

It is fitting to pray at your trade, on a journey, standing at a counter, or sitting at your handicraft.
SAINT JOHN CHRYSOSTOM

Remember...

_____Communicating with God will help you identify his purpose for your life.

_____Prayer provides clarity and helps you avoid missteps and detours.

_____Prayer helps you sort through and discard superficial concerns.

_____Prayer will help you understand and live a simpler lifestyle.

Simplify...

Set aside three minutes for prayer three times a day—morning, noon, and night.

Keep a list of prayer concerns.

In your morning prayer time, pray for clarity and direction for your day.

At noon, offer a prayer of thanksgiving for your blessings.

In your evening prayers, pray for needs and concerns for yourself and others.

There is no place like the feet of Jesus for resolving the problems that perplex our hearts.

G. B. DUNCAN

Right to the Point

Children possess an uncanny ability to cut to the core of the issue, to expose life to the bone, and strip away the barnacles that cling to the hull of our too sophisticated pseudo-civilization.

Gloria Gaither

Jesus had a special bond with children. He often took time to hold them on his lap and bless them. He told his disciples that the key to the kingdom of heaven is to become like those little ones. So what was it that Jesus found so compelling about children and what can you learn about simplifying your life by imitating them?

Perhaps one of the things was that children have the ability to see through superficialities like age, appearance, and social status. They seem to be able to see directly to the essence of the person inside. They don't care that mom is overweight or that dad's hair is thinning or that grandmother has wrinkles or that grandfather can't walk so well. They look at others through the eyes of the heart. The children who sat on Jesus' lap did not rush him with questions or ask him to quell their doubts; they simply believed. Imagine how much simpler life would be if you were to see others in the same way—without bias and preconceived notions.

Children also have a knack for saying what's on their minds. They don't hold back. They speak without pretense. Wouldn't it be nice if adults could abandon nuances and double meanings?

Children don't complicate their communication with God either. They approach God with simple faith and in full assurance that they will be received. Theology and doctrine are issues of little importance to a child. You can walk into God's presence with the same sort of confidence. "Let the little children come to me," Jesus said. "Don't keep them away. God's kingdom belongs to people like them" (Luke 18:16 NIrV).

As you pursue cashing in your hectic lifestyle for a simpler one, avail yourself of the lessons children can teach you.

One Final Thought

Observing children can help you learn important lessons
that will inspire you to get back to basics.

175

Thoughts for Simply Living

Jesus said, "I praise you, Father, Lord of heaven and earth, because you have hidden these things from the wise and learned, and revealed them to little children."

MATTHEW 11:25 NIV

We began by imagining that we are giving to [children]; we end by realizing that they have enriched us.

POPE JOHN PAUL II

Jesus said, "I tell you the truth, anyone who will not receive the kingdom of God like a little child will never enter it."

MARK 10:15 NIV

The heart of a child is the most precious of God's creation.

JOSEPH L. WHITTEN

Remember...

_____God encourages you to adopt the attitude of a small child.

_____God wants you to approach him with boldness, as a child would approach a loving parent.

_____God encourages you to speak with the honesty of a small child.

_____God wants you to come to him just as you are.

Simplify...

Ask a small child about God and see what insight you gain.

Practice seeing past the outside to see who people are on the inside.

Meditate on the question: How is the life of a child simpler than mine?

Read the passages in Matthew, Mark, Luke, and John where Jesus interacts with children.

Begin to address God as your heavenly Father when you pray.

Help us, O God, see your wisdom in the little ones in our midst.

WALTER BRUEGERMANN

Reaching Out

No one is rich enough to do without a neighbor.
Harold Helfer

Jesus led a simple, focused life and yet he placed a high value on fellowship. He walked, talked, and ate with his disciples. His followers gathered together often. He understood that a fellowship of believers bound by love and devotion to God could accomplish much more than many individuals working alone. He wanted his followers to benefit from the strength that comes from depending on one another. He wanted them to see that fellowship simplified their lives by the sharing of resources as each person contributed his or her gift or skill.

This lesson is one that God is eager for his modern-day followers to learn as well. As you walk the Christian walk, you need the strength and talents of others.

Before now, you may have felt that joining a church or becoming part of some other fellowship of believers would be impossible to fit into your busy schedule. But just the opposite is true. The time you invest will quickly be outweighed by the time you save by sharing the gifts and skills of others.

You should keep a few things in mind as you reach out for godly fellowship. First, get to know people for who they are rather than what they do.

Second, prioritize your fellowship with others. Your fellowship with God is most important. Fellowship with your spouse (if you have one) and your children (if you're a parent) come next.

The third thing to remember is to choose friends and companions carefully, because what they say and do will influence your own values and behaviors. Be sure that those you choose to fellowship with share your moral values.

Soon you will find that fellowship is more than just good for you, more than just a way to simpler life; it's God's will for you. Be sure that you place the same value on fellowship that Jesus did.

One Final Thought

Fellowship will help you simplify your life by allowing you to benefit from the gifts and skills of others.

Thoughts for Simply Living

Every day [the believers] continued to meet together in the temple courts. They broke bread in their homes and ate together with glad and sincere hearts, praising God and enjoying the favor of all the people.

ACTS 2:46–47 NIV

The reality of our communion with Christ and in him with one another is the increase of love in our hearts.

WILLIAM TEMPLE

We proclaim to you what we have seen and heard, so that you also may have fellowship with us.

1 JOHN 1:3 NIV

The Bible knows nothing of solitary religion.

JOHN WESLEY

Remember...

_____God created you with an inner longing for fellowship.

_____Fellowship is one of the basic needs of a simple life.

_____Fellowship with God helps you rid yourself of the clutter of everyday living.

_____Fellowship with God will help you see other ways in which to simplify your life.

Simplify...

Look at what you now do alone and ask yourself how you could benefit from the input of others.

Spend an hour with God each Sunday going over the issues of the week.

Choose a specific time to just sit and talk with your spouse.

List some of the resources you could contribute to a fellowship of believers.

Find a church where you feel comfortable and attend at least one function a week.

Christian fellowship is living with and for one another responsibly, that is, in love.

REUEL L. HOWE

181

The Signs Along the Way

On every level of life from housework to heights of prayer, in all judgment and all efforts to get things done, hurry and impatience are sure marks of an amateur.
Evelyn Underhill

*P*atience is more than an aid to simplifying your life; it is a marker to help you judge your progress along the way. Maybe it's a small change that you notice. You no longer feel steamed when your coworker's assistant complicates your too-busy schedule by taking too long at the copier or your son dawdles on his way to the car after school. It seems easier to forbear annoyances when you go after the meat of life.

Increased patience indicates that you are realizing that your job is just your job. You honor God by working hard, doing your best, and showing respect for your employer, but you are no longer driven to get ahead in pursuit of some flimsy, ambiguous standard. You have simplified your attitudes concerning your work.

Showing patience with your family members might indicate that you are growing in your understanding of the value God places on relationships. You can now appreciate with joy the way the sun dances in your son's hair as he walks, stops, and spins his way to the car. You now notice the happiness in his smile, the twinkle in his eyes. You are able to set to memory the wonder of this wonderful gift of parenthood God has given you. Your patience shows that you are now able to appreciate the people God has placed in your life.

As you wait patiently for God's answers to your prayers, you can see that you are gaining a deeper faith and an appreciation for eternal truth and values. You no longer feel compelled to find all the answers. It is enough to trust in God, knowing that he is both loving and faithful.

You are changing from a frantically busy individual running so fast that you miss the true essence of life to a person who is each day growing more centered and balanced and living life as God intended. You are developing patience, and patience is exactly what it will take to reach your goal of a simpler life.

One Final Thought

Patience is a sign, a marker in your journey to find a simpler, more meaningful way of life.

Thoughts for Simply Living

Be joyful in hope, patient in affliction, faithful in prayer.

ROMANS 12:12 NIV

Where there is patience and humility, there is neither anger nor vexation.

SAINT FRANCIS OF ASSISI

Better is the end of a thing than its beginning;
the patient in spirit are better than the proud
in spirit.

ECCLESIASTES 7:8 NRSV

Teach us, O Lord, the disciplines of patience, for to wait is often
harder than to work.

PETER MARSHALL

Remember...

_____God rejoices when he sees you walking in patience.

_____Patience allows you to appreciate the simple, priceless moments in your life.

_____Patience is a sign that you are growing in faith.

_____Patience is an indication that the Holy Spirit is at work in your life.

Simplify...

Pray for patience every day.

Keep track of how many times you exercise patience each day.

Pause to thank God when you feel yourself responding to a certain situation with patience.

Meditate on the blessings that have come to you after a time of patient waiting.

Use patience as a guide to your progress as you take hold of a simpler life.

The principle part of faith is patience.

GEORGE MACDONALD

Simple Living
Simple Blessings

God is more anxious to bestow his blessings on us than we are to receive them.

SAINT AUGUSTINE OF HIPPO

The LORD bless you and keep you; the LORD make his face to shine upon you, and be gracious to you; the LORD lift up his countenance upon you, and give you peace.
NUMBERS 6:24–27 NRSV

Do not pay back evil with evil or cursing with cursing; instead, pay back with a blessing, because a blessing is what God promised to give you when he called you.
1 PETER 3:9 GNT

Blessings crown the head of the righteous.
PROVERBS 10:6 NIV

May the road rise to meet you.

May the wind be always at your back.

May the sun shine warm upon your face.

And the rain fall soft upon your fields.

And until we meet again

May God hold you in the palm of His hand.

IRISH BLESSING

The more you allow God into your daily affairs, the easier you will find it to make the most of your busy day.

Be made new in the attitude of your minds.

EPHESIANS 4:23 NIV

You are the only one who can
decide to simplify your life by
putting your priorities in order.

At Inspirio we love to hear from you—your
stories, your feedback,
and your product ideas.
Please send your comments to us
by way of e-mail at
icares@zondervan.com
or to the address below:

inspirio

Attn: Inspirio Cares
5300 Patterson Avenue SE
Grand Rapids, MI 49530

If you would like further information
about Inspirio and the products we
create, please visit us at:
www.inspiriogifts.com

Thank you and God Bless!

What You Don't Know, That Your Kids Don't Know

What You Don't Know, That Your Kids Don't Know

Roberta Sutton

This book was written to alert both parents and students of the current status of education in the Jefferson County, Colorado School District. It is the opinion of the author that similar environments exist across the nation. Education is important for our children and their futures in this competitive global marketplace. I fear our children will find themselves at a disadvantage, and that is our own fault.

Roberta Sutton's *What You Don't Know, That Your Kids Don't Know*

Copyright 2018 Roberta Sutton.

ISBN – 13: 978-1722987251
ISBN – 10: 1722987251
Library of Congress Control Number: 2018954218
Reed Publishing Ltd.
3719 Evergreen Parkway, Ste. A #36
Evergreen Colorado, 80439
First edition
November, 2018

Dedicated to

The Children of America

Acknowledgements

I would like to thank those who encouraged me to write this book and helped along the way with their advice and editing. You know who you are, and I am deeply grateful for your support and counsel.

"It has become painfully obvious that schools can no longer turn out serious scholars or skilled craftsmen in meaningful numbers when the very basics of education are interspersed and thinned by these damaging experiments.

Phyllis Schlafly

Child Abuse in the Classroom, p. 127

Contents

Foreword

I began substitute teaching for Jefferson County Colorado Public Schools in 2015 after a long hiatus from teaching and subbing. Each evening as I would relate the highlights of my day to my husband, his eyes would get wider and wider in disbelief. A neighbor was often at our house at that time and also heard my accounts. Months later he told my husband: "Roberta needs to write a book, and the name of the book should be *What You Don't Know That Your Kids Don't Know*." When my husband told me, we had a good laugh, but I realized that parents may not really understand the status of the education of their students, since they are fully occupied with working and providing for their families. And even if they are active in their students' school, they may not have noticed how things have changed. After all, I have been nearly all day in a teacher's classroom before noticing some obvious but unusual things.

This little book is merely the observations of a single substitute teacher during a very limited time in this position. I make no claim that this will be a researched or exhaustive study of the subject. It is mostly written from my point of view. Where that is not the case, you will be able to tell. With that disclaimer, you may want to stop reading now. But I hope you won't. Some of the things I observed may be instructive to you and in some way may benefit your children. This encompasses Middle Schools and High Schools in the Jefferson County Colorado School District. The subjects were math, science, English, and

1

history (social studies). Jefferson County is a lovely westerly suburb of Denver, Colorado. Although you may not live in my area, I believe our school district is representative of much of the country.

School days are the time for teaching young children a body of essential knowledge—while at the same time inspiring them to look beyond—to realize the next innovative miracle is waiting and can be envisioned. But this knowledge acquired during school days is crucial. It's actually their arsenal to face issues in adult life.

A bit about my vantage point: in my high school years (in the 1950s) school was generally considered a happy experience—replete with worthy academics to ponder and enjoy; athletic teams, and all the other ancillary aspects that make school something to look forward to each day. Academics were broken down into presented lessons that were age-appropriate and length-of-time-allotted-appropriate too, so that there was a sense of accomplishment each day and a feeling of being in good hands. Lessons were learned along a straight line of progress in most classes. Students usually went home each day with a sense of accomplishment and the assurance that there were plans by their teachers for presenting them with the needed body of knowledge that had been accumulated by scholars through the ages, and that they would need to know to be able to carry on after graduation.

I make no pretense at being an education expert, but I feel this will be a look into a world you can no longer enter, or, if you do, may not fully comprehend, with only a short and cursory investigation. In many cases I did not realize what I was seeing until I had been sitting in the

2

classroom through several class periods. We are all so programmed to believe school is as we remember it from a former time, that we are not looking for differences.

This book is in no way a disparagement of the Jefferson County School System or its teachers. In fact, I believe Jefferson County schools to be among the best public schools in the country. The point I will be making is the general departure nation-wide from what many of us think of as education. There has been a change in *philosophy and culture*, and it has been so gradual that it has gone undetected. This new philosophy is taught in our teachers' colleges. "Direct Instruction" is out of favor, as you will see as this book unfolds.

Another experience a few years ago also spurred me to write this book. Tom Tancredo, while he was our Congressman in Washington, addressed a women's luncheon. He related a story about a conversation he had with a constituent. This gentleman's son was about to graduate from high school. The family was very proud of him; he had taken all the difficult classes and had good grades. After dinner, as a manner of making conversation, the father asked his son to tell him all the things he knew about George Washington. He expected his son to start reeling off lots of details that he himself didn't know. Instead, there was silence; and then more silence. Finally the son said: "Well, I know he had slaves." The father was dumbfounded. His son didn't know about Washington's leading his country to victory against the most powerful nation in the world, or presiding over the Constitutional Convention. And of course there is so much more.

Many of us think school is like it was when we were in school, or at least when our grown children were in school. Neither is true. The changes have not been in a positive direction. And you should absolutely know! People say: "I want my child to be socialized," thinking sending them to school will do that, and that it is going to be a positive influence. You may want to think about that again.

5

PART I

CHAPTER 1

My Direct Experiences

I am an insider in today's public schools. I want to take you on a journey that will be enlightening—and probably shocking.

Although I was a full-time physics, chemistry, and math teacher for some years, I am presently an active substitute teacher in the Jefferson County, Colorado public schools. As a substitute, I teach a variety of classes—and I get more than a glimpse of what is being taught. You may be surprised at what you don't know, and what your kids don't know. It's a different world than you think. I have heard parents say, "I don't even try to keep up with my kids' homework—they teach so differently these days."

I subbed for a seventh grade English class and the work for the class period was like this: the teacher had provided a worksheet for the students (enough for half the class, so they had to share). They sat at tables, two on a side. It showed a picture of a pop can that was dented. The instructions were: you are a pop can that has been popped, drunk, squished, and thrown away. You are now lying on your therapist's couch and telling the therapist

how it feels to be a pop can that has been popped, drunk, squished, and thrown away. Aside from a little bit of free reading at the beginning of class, that assignment consumed the whole class period. It was a content-free assignment. And there were no English text books that I could find in the room. The free reading I just mentioned was not at the teacher's direction. It was totally FREE reading. Many were reading comic books.

In the same 7th grade English class (on another day), the students were putting the finishing touches on a paper due that day, which was a Friday. They had worked on it all week. The paper consisted of analyzing their names. This entailed identifying the person who named them, if their first names were family names, if they liked their first names, and the country origin of the last names. This was a week-long project. Again, there was no content regarding English literature or grammar.

English class can be bright with learning grammar points and specimens of our fabulous literature. I don't believe any of the students had ever heard the words "conjugate a verb." I'm not sure they knew what "tenses" meant, and that the form of the verb changes with the tense, or if they knew about the three principle parts of a verb. We have the richest language in the world with 600,000 words—60,000 in common use. They not only need to know words, but how to pronounce them, their meanings, and how to spell them. (Spell Check can only go so far—if you're not close to the right spelling, it's useless.)

Besides, they need to be taught the zest and excitement of learning beautiful, precise, and interesting words. There are funny things to be shared too – such as

Spoonerisms, named after the famous Cambridge professor at the turn of the 20th century, the Reverend Dr. William Archibald Spooner.

Our English teacher read us Spoonerisms and would have us practically rolling on the floor with laughter. She read us recipes in Spoonerism. (It was a special treat the last few minutes on Friday if we'd worked hard all week.) In case you don't know what a Spoonerism is, I'll give my favorite: being a Reverend, he officiated at wedding ceremonies. At the conclusion of one he said, "It is kisstomary to cuss the bride." I'll add another: to a student he said, "You've tasted the whole worm." (You've wasted the whole term.) The poor professor did it spontaneously, and was so embarrassed by it, but his students at the university loved it.

But I digress! Mortimer Adler said: "The goods of the mind are information, knowledge, understanding, and wisdom." School is one place that should furnish those goods.

In a seventh grade social studies class, the teacher had given the students the job of making up an imaginary country. They were to name it, make up a language for it, and name that language, make an alphabet, and draw a physical map of the country which would include its shape and where its rivers and mountains and lakes were. They also had to make a political map of their country where they showed the states (or counties). They had to color it with colored pencils. They were to staple the two sheets together and turn them in on Friday (the day I was there).

There is an immense amount of information to know about the world! There are the mighty rivers of the world

to learn and the mountain ranges. It would be interesting to understand its peoples gathered into different countries—how those different people dressed; how the countries supported themselves—mining—agriculture— commerce on the ocean; how they governed themselves (political systems). Again, there was no content in this assignment (lots of fanciful imagining). And again, there were no visible books in use. The students could use the chrome books (mini computers which are like iPads) furnished by the school.

It was my pleasure to sub for a high school calculus class. There was some really good teaching going on there. The teacher had the students so well instructed that they came in and got right to work. They did have books—and I believe the students had the books checked out to them for the year. They were surprised I knew a little bit about calculus. This teacher didn't allow any food in the classroom. A girl, to her credit, asked if she could finish her roll—that it was her breakfast. I had to say no. The rules can't be mutable just because there is a substitute.

Speaking of math, I did some subbing in sixth grade math. That is where I made a really surprising discovery that has nothing to do with math. The teacher had left us a worksheet (a kind of a puzzle) where the students had to work a problem and then look for the answer in a numbered box on the sheet that was the "Key" to get the letter that corresponded with the answer. They then put that letter that matched the answer in a series of numbered boxes at the bottom of the sheet. When they finished filling in the boxes at the bottom, it created a phrase.

As I was strolling around observing the students' work, I noticed a little boy who had just matched an answer with a letter, and he had to put that letter at the bottom in the numbered spaces. The letter was a "P." I was so surprised at how he wrote the P, that I said: "Has no one ever shown you how to make a P?" He looked at me startled. Then we both burst out laughing—as did the other students in earshot. The way he made a P was to start at the bottom and go up and then loop around. I do realize that students only print—cursive having been dropped from the curriculum several years ago—but for some reason I had supposed the elementary teachers would have devoted themselves even more diligently to making sure the students' printing was clear and the order and direction of the strokes was followed. After that incident, I made it a point to look at the "handwriting" of students of all grades. I was and am so dismayed at what I saw. Not only did the students not have a foundation of writing (printing); but the way they held a pencil was inconvenient, and not ergonomic.

In earlier periods we were taught to hold the pencil with the thumb, index finger, and third finger—the third finger, with its strength, guiding the writing. I didn't know a single person who didn't write that way. I believe it to be ergonomically the best. Today the students often put two fingers on the top of the pencil shaft and guide with the fourth finger. I noticed that in timed class work the students had a hard time finishing. They were struggling so hard to write (print). They are slowed down terribly by this one small change. (Some students put three or even four fingers on top of the shaft of the pencil.) Also, when students don't have down pat the order and direction of the printing strokes, then the writing is like drawing and

consequently much slower.   I also noticed at all grades that the students use mostly the capital letters.

Previously, elementary schools taught printing in first and second grades.   In the third grade they taught handwriting, and anchored it in fourth grade. There used to be Penmanship Competitions. There is definitely not a penmanship competition in schools these days! (Penmanship was striving for beauty in our writing.)

In another middle school, as I was speaking with a Special Ed teacher, I pointed out the odd way some of the students were holding their pencils. He said he'd been teaching since 1995 and had never noticed it before. But a friend who is a retired elementary school teacher, and who subs occasionally, was distraught by what she was seeing. She told me that you have to catch this issue in pre-school in order to teach students to hold the pencil with three fingers—that they almost can't change later.

More information about the abandonment of cursive: Michael Hairston, President of the Fairfax Education Association, the largest teachers' union in the country, called cursive "a dying art."   He continues—"Cursive writing is a traditional skill that has been replaced with technology. ...Educators are having to make choices about what they teach with a limited amount of time."[1] Since 2010, 45 states adopted the Common Core standards, which do not include cursive instruction.

Back to the math class: there was a need for some computing. They needed to add 2-digit numbers. Many students were very inattentive to aligning the numbers one directly under the other, which made it very difficult to add the numbers. These were sixth graders who

should have, by that time, seen the need for attention to that important detail.

In this same class, although they were only sixth graders, everybody had a cell phone. I noticed one boy's cell phone had a completely smashed screen. When I mentioned it, he laughed and said that he had stomped on it, but that his father would buy him another one.

Eating in class is a big issue these days. This also was a 6th grade class, and the time was near the Christmas vacation. All the students had been given candy canes that morning. They loved them so much, and they claimed they couldn't put them down because it would make the desk sticky and their hands were already sticky. I could see that was the case. Not many papers came in that day. There is eating in virtually all classes; middle school and high school. The students are allowed to eat anytime they want. Often eating takes precedence over the work of the day. They complain they are very hungry. Eating was always allowed except in that one calculus class I mentioned.

When subbing in a high school chemistry class, I sat in the room nearly all day before my curiosity was aroused as to what was lining the ledge behind the counters of three of the walls of the chemistry room. They looked like stuffed animals—crudely made. I asked a girl in the last period what they were. She told me that they had been studying Moles earlier, and the teacher had all her students go home and fashion and make a mole (the animal).

In case you might not know, the concept of Mole in chemistry is a number—6.02×10^{23} —just like the word "dozen" stands for 12. It's a shame that scientists chose a

name for Mole that already had a meaning. What chemistry teachers try to do is to disconnect the image of the animal and replace it with the chemistry concept. A Mole is the number of molecules in an atomic weight of a substance. This teacher had done exactly the confusing thing. Besides that, there was the time and effort of her students going to the store, buying the fabric, and stitching together the little stuffed animals and painting on eyes and whiskers, etc.—a craft project—for senior high students! There is so much chemistry to teach and so many good labs to do. This class didn't have books either.

Another high school is offering a special program to prepare students to go into the medical lab profession. The students can sign up for it at the beginning of their 9th grade year. It is aimed at producing workers who, upon graduating from high school, can walk right into a medical lab and get a job. This is a skill. This may sound good to you. But is it education? Grooming and empowering a mind is different from a skill. This may sound good to those who are out of a job and want their kids not to be, but preparing kids for a world workforce is a socialistic concept where the broader mentality is ignored. Preparing an elastic mind with knowledge, enabling students to adapt to lots of situations, is more what I mean by "education."

In one of the middle schools where I taught, a regular eighth grade physical science class is now called "Engineering." The students are quite proud of themselves for taking engineering—though, in my opinion, they know fewer scientific facts than are part of

a traditional physical science class. I've taught a lot of eighth grade physical science.

One of my most interesting subbing days was at a high school for one of the physics teachers. I was delighted since that subject was my college major. The room looked like a physics room, but I found out things operate differently now.

The students came in and got settled at their tables. They went to the chrome book cart and brought the chrome books to their places. After logging in on Schoology, they got their teacher's lesson of several problems for the day and began working on them. He had left an answer sheet for them to check their work.

They were studying the most difficult section of physics called "mechanics." This is the section of physics where you are taught equations involving speed, velocity, acceleration, force, momentum, mass, pressure, etc. There were small "personal size" white boards and markers for the students to use to work out the problems, rather than use paper. They all worked together at the tables. They emailed in their answers to the problems, and toward the end of the period, proceeded to put the chrome books back and left at the bell.

After sitting there all day, I began to look around the room. Someone had posted a small sign on a wall that said: "SUCKS, TO BE YOU." By the teacher's desk were several smaller posters of well-known football players— all with the teacher's face photo-shopped on them.

During the final period I asked some girls where the physics books were, and they said they didn't use any books. I'm sure my face registered surprise. I asked if

their teacher did everything with handouts. They said no; that the teacher didn't believe in paper. The girls said he had only stood up in front of the class and taught them two times so far that year, and I was there well into the school year. I remember from my own experience learning physics as a student in high school and in college, having had to read a paragraph five times before the concept being taught was clear. The girls said that they didn't know what they were doing. They were memorizing and using formulas without having them derived in front of them at the board.

In a high school history (social studies) class, they *did* have textbooks. I noticed George Washington's name was mentioned on three pages of the textbook. I don't know if the other Founders were included. I also noticed that most of the texts were highlighted by the students in multiple colors of highlights—this was more than just pencil underlining and writing in the margins. Some of the blue highlights made the print almost illegible. Formerly, school books were to be kept in as pristine a condition as possible for the future classes that used them.

In that same class was an exchange student from Italy. She had a beautiful accent, but spoke very good English. I asked her if it was hard to keep up since the classes were in a foreign language. She said she worked hard, but that most of the classes were rather easy, for which she was grateful.

In a middle school science class we did use textbooks for the assignment. The students said, however, that they had not worked their way up to that point in the book. It was just an assignment chosen at random by the teacher.

On the subject of textbook use, my feeling is that if you have a fine text book and a student works his way through it, there is a sense of accomplishment because he has covered all the material in that book. The student actually knows where an idea is brought up and can look back to find it.

In a high school History/Government class the teacher had me show a YouTube film by John Stossel on the subject "Is America Number One?" It addressed all the major aspects of a culture—economic stability, how the poor are treated, religious freedom, freedom of expression—that sort of thing. America's shortcomings were brought forth (with interviews from the darkest ghettos including people of all lifestyles and beliefs), and America's good points. Then they included the pros and cons of other cultures. It was abundantly clear that America, with all its faults, did the best job of governance. The students filled out a survey at the end of each class period. Out of 57 students, six answered NO to the question "Is America better?" Very interesting!

One thing you may not have realized is that memorization is frowned upon. It is called second class learning—deriving ideas from their rudiments is considered better. So, in many schools the memorization of the multiplication tables isn't stressed. Even important math formulas aren't to be memorized. Poetry and famous speeches aren't memorized. Many of us feel that these items are necessary things for your "toolbox" to carry into life.

I recently asked an English teacher if she corrected her students' work. She assured me she certainly did. I asked if she corrected speech—when the person might make an

error in pronunciation or perhaps in syntax: like "him and me" where it should be "he and I", or the often mispronounced word "anyway" which should have no "s" on the end, and "these ones"—where it should be just "these." She said that she did not do that; it might offend the person. But a student would learn so quickly if there were correction at the time. It makes such an impact to be shown the right way when you've just made an error. All the red ink laboriously lavished on submitted papers often is for naught. I believe most students look at the grade and only give a passing glance to the corrections.

In one of the middle schools where I was called to teach, I was happy to see that I would be leading a science lab that day. When I got there I was surprised to see that we were to leave the class room, which WAS a science lab room with sinks, and scientific equipment, to go upstairs to the computer lab. That was the kind of lab they meant. The whole experiment (including stirring a beaker of boiling water and taking the temperature of the water, etc.) was done on the computer screen. There was no hands-on experimentation. It was a virtual lab! Again, no books—just a handout. I believe there is no replacement for hands-on experiential learning.

In a high school English class the students were supposed to pick a piece of literature (a poem), and make what amounts to a power-point presentation including music. This was a good computer class exercise, but the English literature aspect of it was nearly non-existent. In that school the only person who knew how to add music to a power point was a lady in the library. She was over worked since all types of classes were working on computer assignments. After she was requested to come

to the computer lab room, the students in that class just sat there and waited for her to show up—which she didn't! I do believe students need to learn to use computers, but what we have traditionally thought of as a classical education where students are treated to great ideas and the active "life of the mind," is being sacrificed on the altar of becoming more computer proficient. Computer work should be taught, yes, but it should be a class led by a competent tech person. Students could make much more rapid gains if that were the focus. I'm beginning to think that substitute *"subject matter"* teachers aren't needed—just IT people. It seems electronics is getting between the teacher and the student.

Books that students read are important. During the time when any of us reads a book, the plot and the tone of it is a part of our thought. Selections should be suggested that enlighten us with wisdom. In one school certain books were being advertised with posters on the inside walls of bathroom doors—of all places! All these books seemed to me to be depressing: *The Fault in Our Stars* is about Hazel and her cancer support group. She falls in love and then dies. Others were *Shatter Me*, and *Juliette's Touch Was Fatal*. *We Were Liars* is about four friends who were liars. These are books where despair is the fashion. That dark tone seemed to be prevalent in many schools. Another one I saw advertised in another school in the same manner (inside the door of a stall in the girl's restroom) was *I Was Here,* by Gayle Forman. The summary said it is about two girlfriends in high school. One goes off to college in another city and commits suicide. The other girl goes to the city to try to find out what happened. (Again, terribly dark.)

A recent article by Steve Salerno entitled "The Unbearable Darkness of Young Adult Literature" related his experience attending the inaugural Summit on the "Research and Teaching of Young Adult Literature," held at the University of Nevada, Las Vegas in June (2018). It featured books on "sexual abuse, dysphoria, racism, gang life, domestic violence, and school shootings." He observed: "It is difficult to understand why educators would so determinedly insist on immersing student in an unsavory worldview, portraying life in terms of its anomalies and unorthodoxies, as if there's something wrong with you if there's nothing wrong with you." He quoted one teacher participant who said: "I feel privileged to have been a part of this historic event." His article ended with: "Perhaps they should consider recommending books that make the world sound like a more hospitable place to be."[2]

In several English class rooms I saw a book I became concerned about—called *The Bluest Eye*. It was on the bookshelves of several schools. I googled it to see what it was about. It's a book that raises questions of racism, incest, molestation, pedophilia, etc. Students use these books for their free reading. The appearance of a book on a classroom bookshelf implies endorsement from the school, or at least from the teacher. This book is so objectionable that I don't think it belongs in middle schools or high schools at all.

In a ninth grade English class the students were studying *Lord of the Flies* by William Golding. I realize this is considered a "classic." In case you haven't read it, it is a picture of degeneracy and of man's lowest nature—and that it comes forth if he is left to his own means—without

society. In other words, it's saying that man is basically bad. The little boys who are castaways become savages except for three of them, and two of them are killed before a navy cruiser finds them. This may be appropriate for college—but 9th graders?

Parents need to be aware of what their children are viewing as well as reading—especially with the surge of student suicide today. Oprah Winfrey said a wise thing. She said that she doesn't watch horror films because she can't un-see them. All of us probably should be more selective about what we voluntarily allow into our consciousness.

At this same high school I subbed for a history teacher and when I went to the history department workroom to eat my lunch, there on the back wall I saw a huge poster of Karl Marx as well as a poster of Ché Guevara. I'm sure everyone knows Marx was the father of Communism (having written the *Communist Manifesto*). Guevara is from Argentina, and figures hugely in the Cuban Revolution. His visage has become a counter culture symbol of revolution. Why these were on the wall in an American high school, I can't imagine. On the inside of the door of that same room were a couple of posters— "Happiness comes from within—that's why it feels so good to fart," and "There are electrons, protons, and neutrons. They left out morons."

At a middle school I sat in for a teacher whose planning period was at the first of the school day. I was looking for the books to see what students were doing. A helpful next-door teacher stopped in to say hello, so I asked her where the books were. Her answer astonished me. She said, "Oh, at our school, we have all our books in the

library." I asked, "Do you mean even the textbooks?" She said, "Yes." If the student wants to check out a book the student has to go to the library to check it out. None were used in the classroom—there weren't any—not even a class set. I believe the teacher handled the classes with handouts, which means she is making up the course as she goes. A neighbor teacher said the course curriculum was a work in progress.

At another middle school I was surprised to see the room's ceiling decorated with models of the earth that the students had made using a balloon and papier-mâché. They were painted, depicting the water and land areas. It was in celebration of Earth Day. (Earth Day happens to be celebrated on April 22, Lenin's birthday.) The worshipping of mother earth didn't used to be a part of the curriculum. It is a waste of time for students to have to do a craft project when there is so much to learn in social studies/history/geography. There isn't much learning in making a model.

It was close to Thanksgiving, so I told the students the remarkable story of the pilgrims and about Squanto—and that Squanto was English speaking—and how that came about. The teacher was back in the classroom by that time, sitting at his desk. He listened with rapt attention, not knowing the story either. Students love stories; it's how most of us learn—having pictures painted in our thoughts. Speaking of that, in most cases, I don't get a chance to contribute anything from myself to the class. I truly am a glorified roll taker!

When subs go to a school at the start of the day, we go to the office and sign in. We get a key, the substitute teacher's reporting sheet that must be filled out, and a

lanyard to go around the neck identifying a substitute teacher in the building.

At one school an additional thing is given—a list of students who must not be allowed out of the classroom during the period. I called it "The No Fly List." The secretary explained to me that if any student on this long list needed to leave the classroom for any reason (bathroom, drink, etc.), I was to call the main office (phones are on every teacher's desk) and request an escort for the No Fly person. They would be escorted to the bathroom (or wherever) and be brought back. These students had been identified as "runners." If they left the classroom they wouldn't be back. They would leave the school grounds.

This reminds me of another odd thing I've noted. The incidence of going to the bathroom or getting a drink is very high—probably an average of 12 times in a class period. A few decades ago, leaving the room to visit the bathroom was rare—an emergency. It was virtually unheard of, to get a drink.

On the bright side, at the same high school, I subbed for a math teacher who actually made use of the smartboard in her room—which is a computer the teacher can program. She had prepared a lesson—complete not only with the problems for the day, but she worked out some illustration problems. She then had handouts for the problems. Her students worked well, but again, no books.

About the smartboards: we subs were not given instruction on how to use them. Judging from what the students told me some teachers also didn't know clearly how to use them—and didn't use them for their intended

purpose. I called the sub office shortly after starting to sub, to see if I could come in for a demonstration. I was told nothing like that existed. Usually the smartboards are used to show videos—a big screen for the videos which are run on the teacher's computer tower by the teacher's desk.

In a high school English class, I was surprised that a fellow was sitting there doing nothing on the assignment. When I asked him, he said he didn't have a pencil. I gave him one, but I joked with him that his excuse was one a second grader would use. I encouraged him to come equipped, take charge, bring extra of everything each day. (High school kids shouldn't have to be told that.)

Many students are embarrassed to admit they don't "get it." One boy in a high school math class was hunched over his math paper most of the period. I thought he was working away. Come to find out, he was erasing as he went along because he didn't understand what he was doing and wanted to look busy. He didn't have one problem done. He said he was totally lost. This was supposedly a type of work the teacher had explained. My heart melted, because I know the desperate feeling. It only took a couple of sentences to make it clear, and he got right to work and did a good job of the assignment. Math is an area where you don't dare have holes in your understanding—you cannot go forward with gaps in knowledge.

I subbed in an 8th grade science class where the teacher had left a movie for the students to see—a fabulous movie about the universe. It moved very fast. Even if you wanted to take notes, you couldn't unless you watched it several times. It was far over the kids' heads and they

quickly lost interest. It would have been appropriate for a college level class in astronomy. The kids were so disengaged and distraught, that they were getting out of their seats, noisy, and one boy was putting sticky notes all over his face. The age appropriateness of the day's work needs to be front and center in choosing what is presented to students, otherwise the time is wasted and worse than that, the students get a "bad taste" for that class or subject, or for school in general. I have found that where the classwork is appropriate, both in length and in difficulty, students like doing it—they thrive on it. Where work assigned is outside those bounds, however, there is frustration and rebellion

I subbed in another physics class. The students in this gentleman's physics classes were utterly delightful. They were doing a lab the day I was there, but again it was a virtual lab having to do with studying light and waves. In the past, each lab group would set up a ripple tank complete with two sources for generating waves—in order to observe how the two outgoing waves interfered with each other, causing nodes (where the two sets of waves cancel out each other). Kids love seeing this—where there are smooth spots (nodes) whereas all around, there are waves; also, how waves bend around barriers, etc.

The on-line version loaded extremely slowly, and on some computers it didn't load at all. Some students didn't even get to start the lab. This only confirms my belief that a hands-on experiment—using actual lab equipment—is worth the time and energy to set up the equipment, which takes about half the class period. I should clarify—a virtual lab isn't one where someone performing the lab

is videoed, and you watch him do the lab—but it is totally virtual. It is more on the order of a video game.

In this same physics room I counted 238 physics books not in use. Students are instead using a manual-style book which comes in two parts—one for 1st semester and one for 2nd semester. The manual has some text, but is comprised mostly of problems. It's more like a workbook. Of the texts mentioned, one title had 114 books. That would be enough for all of his students in all his classes to have the same book. He taught around 90 students. Using textbooks seems to be out of fashion.

There is a proliferation of science classes. Here is a list of offerings at the above-mentioned school: Conceptual Chemistry, Regular Chemistry, Honors Chemistry, AP Chemistry, AP Environmental Science, AP Biology, Anatomy and Physiology (Honors), Marine Biology, Biotechnology Engineering (Honors), Astronomy, Forensic Science, Physics, Honors Physics, Engineering Design and Development, Principles of Engineering, and Natural Science. It sounds like a college catalog. Formerly just biology, chemistry, and physics were taught. We did well to pass all three with good understanding.

In this same physics class I was observing a boy typing on his computer. I noticed he didn't use his fourth fingers or his little fingers. I asked him if he had studied typing. He said they had it in 4th grade; one day every week for a part of the day. The teacher had shown them where to put their fingers and to use their thumb for the space bar. I asked him if he could type without looking at his fingers. He said no. So the "touch typing" we used to learn, where typing students stared straight ahead at the keyboard chart on the wall (our keys were blank—no

letters) isn't generally taught anymore. So much has changed!

It was in a middle school 8th grade math class that I had a revelation. I call it the "calculator vs. fractions" dilemma. I had a delightful day sitting in for a math teacher. The students were great. The revelation came as I was driving home—the reason why these students didn't understand fractions was because they had calculators. Calculators don't understand fractions. Everything is decimal. It cemented my belief that students shouldn't be allowed to use calculators until at least algebra I. Students need to be able to calculate before they have a device to use that is intended to speed up calculations.

If the fractions given in a problem can be written easily as decimals, there isn't much of a problem. But fractions can be anything—and sometimes the actual answer needs to be written as a fraction in order to be exact. This is where calculators, that turn everything into decimals, can be a hindrance.

When the students first started working on their worksheet they were grasping the calculators and looking at them as if they expected the device to save them from this assignment. These calculators were on their desks— furnished by the school. I am sure that decision was well intentioned, but it tends to cripple thinking especially when the day's work is on fractions.

While teaching math at one of our high schools I made another discovery—that our high school students can no longer do long division—if they ever could. (Some students said they never learned—that they moved around a lot and missed it everywhere.) The hardest

problem that came up for them to do was to divide 124 by 2. To his credit, the regular teacher didn't permit calculators nor the calculator feature on their iPhones. When they reached the division problem most of them could do the division in their heads, but as I was strolling around, I saw that some of the students were having trouble with that division problem. I told them to set it up as a long division problem and do it that way. Some looked at me blankly and some told me they had never learned how, as mentioned above. These students were unfamiliar with the divide symbol where the number to be divided went under the symbol and the divisor went in front (the way earlier generations learned it). Students learn this in about 4th grade. I wondered what they would have done if the numbers had been larger. Calculators are doing our students a disservice since, when they are taken away, the students are left floundering.

Our students even have trouble with subtraction (or making change). This reminds me of a time when a friend gave a $10.00 bill to a young lady at a business. The charge was $7.50. She apologized as she was getting out her calculator to see what the change should be. She said: "I just don't trust myself to give the right change." She was a recent high school graduate.

By the way, the calculator app. on your iPhone does have an important use. Did you know that when you pull up the calculator app. on your phone (where you can add, subtract, multiply, and divide), that when you turn the phone sideways, all the other functions come up? There you will find square roots, cube roots, sin, cos, tan, etc. Since the trigonometry function tables have been removed from the backs of trig. books, students will need

a math calculator or their iPhone to get these values. The cell phone is really a computer with a phone app.!

A lady in the school office at the end of the school day to whom I mentioned this disheartening discovery about long division, quipped "I guess it's just a sign of the times." That is obviously true, but our children of today should not be less able and knowledgeable than their parents.

After noticing the problem with long division, I did some checking. A current elementary school teacher enlightened me about Common Core's math program. Under current Jeffco math curriculum, it is possible that students never encounter the "long division" with which we are familiar. They learn to divide using more conceptual/regrouping methods. Common Core has multiple ways of arriving at an answer. In Jefferson County, long division is taught in 3rd grade and repeated in 4th grade—and it is taught using a few methods as mentioned above, called algorithms. Even the method taught a couple of generations ago is called an algorithm—though I never heard that term used for it. It isn't taught, however.

Even very good math students often get the wrong answer using some of these algorithms, but the third grade teacher said that the answer is considered all right if it is close. I'm dumbfounded to think a wrong answer on a math problem can be considered all right if it is close! (We would have missed the moon!)

A gentleman who was on the Math Validation Committee to write Common Core Math, Dr. James Milgram, a math professor at Stanford at the time, refused to sign off on

the Common Core Standards. Other members of the committee did the same. What Common Core did was to make it relatively difficult for people to find the names of the five or six members of the Committee who dissented. The original project was represented to them asserting that Common Core was first rate and internationally benchmarked. Milgram's comment was that neither claim was true, and Common Core has since removed the claim of international benchmarking from its website. Dr. Milgram is now retired, and is an Emeritus Professor at Stanford. He was the only one in the group who was actually a mathematics professor.

Wrap up

To wrap up my sentiments about my recent subbing experiences, I do realize how very easy it is to find fault. I also realize that some of the teachers I have sat in for were intentionally leaving me with what they hoped would be an easy day of teaching. Probably the things I've observed were not of their doing or choice. I have intentionally not mentioned names of teachers or schools. That's not my purpose. The unions play a bigger part in directing the schools activities than any of us realizes. However, the teachers themselves are taught to think along new lines in their college courses these days. Many are young and thoroughly believe that the new direction that education is heading is great. Many of us on the outside, however, see problems.

CHAPTER 2

Experiences Others Have Shared With Me

Shortly after I stopped my full-time teaching to start a family, a teacher friend also left the school where we had taught together. Even though we were both teaching science, she actually was a math teacher who was capable of teaching the highest high school math classes. She went to one of the Aurora high schools. We kept in touch in the summer time—getting together for lunch. At first she was very happy to be teaching in her major field, and teaching all the top math classes at her high school. As the summers rolled on, though, she was discouraged that some advanced math classes had been dropped. I guess students weren't signing up. It ended up that eventually all the higher math classes were dropped.

One of the premier high schools in Jefferson County opened in 1973. As I remember, the school offered Greek, Latin, German, Spanish, and French foreign languages. The classes were all flourishing. At present the offerings are French, German and Spanish—which is still good. However, in a foreign language department, the presence of Latin or Greek is a good barometer of the intellectual rigor of the school.

Back in the 1990s a science teacher told me a sad story. He taught earth science, a course 9th graders all took. He said he'd taught 33 years and couldn't wait to retire. Here is one of the reasons why. He had given one of his students, a girl, a "C" in his class for the first quarter grading period. He didn't actually give it to her, it's what she earned. Her mother made an appointment for a conference. When she came she said: "What do you mean by giving my daughter a "C" in your class? She has always been a straight "A" student." So he turned his grade book around (back in the days of a paper grade book) and offered for her to see her daughter's grades. She said she didn't want to look, and that she didn't care about that. He looked at her astonished and said: "Well, what do you want me to do?" She said: "Well, change the grade, of course." He changed it to an "A." I asked him why, and he said he knew he wouldn't get any backup from the administration. He was close to retirement and didn't want to jeopardize his pension.

I personally had an interesting experience when a daughter took French in 9th grade. She kept coming home and saying they weren't learning anything. I brushed it off thinking she meant they weren't working very hard in class. In about October she brought home a cassette tape with a class period recorded on it. (Another student had brought in a small tape recorder, and our daughter had borrowed the tape.) There was absolutely not a word of French on it. The class discussed movies and movie stars. As we all listened to it, she said: "Now do you believe me?" I told her I did, and could she get me another mother to go in with me to talk to the principal. She got me two.

Armed with our tape, we sat down with the principal, and the first thing he said was that he could not listen to it—that it violated employer and employee relationship in the union contract, and that there was nothing he could do since she had tenure. He said she would be retiring in two years. Our students dropped the class at semester. The principal said he'd wondered why so many of her students dropped at semester in the past.

Another daughter during her sixth grade year told me an interesting story. The teacher had given the class their 20 spelling words to learn for the week. One of this daughter's friends asked the teacher for more words, since she'd already learned the first list. The teacher replied: "Learn to spell them backwards."

Some of you may remember the only time in the recent past that a school board tried to fire a teacher. He was a high school English teacher in Jefferson County. He showed a film yearly, *1900*, that was rated "R". Perhaps that was the proper rating at that time, but from reading the description of it, the rating should have been XXX. It showed oral sex, frontal nudity, cocaine abuse, graphic violence, and was filled with foul language. Teachers can show films like that if they give the proper disclosure to parents, and get their approval for the viewing, and allow students to opt out. He seemed to be quite remiss, in that he never took time to get permission from parents.

One year a student told her parents about it. The parents reported it to the administration, and proceedings commenced. Come to discover, the school administration was wishing for a way to replace him. He apparently rarely attended faculty meetings, was usually 15 minutes late to his classes, didn't keep appointments made with

parents, and rarely sent down an attendance slip for the class periods. The upshot is that the teacher joined the Union—Jefferson County Education Association (JCEA) in order to get the legal defense they provide. He was brought to trial, and the School Board lost. It was appealed and while waiting, he got his salary, though not teaching. The School Board won on appeal and he did lose his job. It took about two years—one for each trial, and cost an enormous amount of money. That is why the school district (so strictly constrained by the Union), hardly ever attempts to fire a teacher. Instead we have what is called "The Dance of the Lemons." Poor teachers are transferred from school to school. More on that later.

In another vein, on September 26, 2017, a talk show host on 710 KNUS radio in Denver, related the story of a girl who plays volleyball. At a school she visited for a game, there was a chart on the wall of the gym. It listed good qualities and bad qualities of an athlete. Under the "Bad" category was "Religious."

You may not know if your child isn't college age yet, but remedial courses are a big deal for colleges/universities now. This wasn't the case in the past. Those remedial courses didn't exist, or were extremely rare. You may want to check when your son/daughter heads off to college to see if the college is happy with their high school transcript, or if they will require remediation. Usually math is the major consideration. These classes don't count toward graduation, but they do cost tuition.

When a high school in Jeffco needed to add an English teacher for the following year, the interview committee interviewed teachers who were English majors—some just finished with college. When they came to the

question "How do you feel about diagramming sentences?" nearly all said they had never diagrammed a sentence. The committee ended up hiring an older teacher who liked the process. Diagramming sentences is considered by many to be the most efficient way of teaching grammar.

Here's another story Tom Tancredo, our former U.S. Congressman, told recently. He was asked to speak at an assembly in the auditorium of a brand new high school. When he got there he was graciously given a tour of this large state-of-the-art high school. Later that day, in the assembly, elated by what he had seen of this beautiful school, he opened his remarks to the not-quite filled auditorium. The students were seated, and the teachers/administration stood along the sides of the auditorium. He said: "Is this a great country or what— that you have such a great facility!" He expected the kids to be smiling and nodding their heads or giving a thumbs up. But instead they looked down, and then looked over at their teachers. He was shocked.

A friend of mine said his granddaughter asked him to take her to the IMAX program on the Second World War. He was happy to do it, and as they were driving he asked her why exactly she chose that. She said that she didn't know much about the Second World War and wanted to learn more. So he asked her what she had been taught in school about it. She said all she knew was that America was the only country ever to have dropped the atom bomb.

According to a post by band teacher, Mary Mackie, our high School bands are out-of-fashion in some areas. Its members are thought of as "band geeks". Those other

students probably have no idea how much time and effort goes into learning how to make that instrument sound good, how hard it is to march (parades and football half-times) and play an instrument at the same time. Also there is the cost of buying an instrument or renting it, and the cost of purchasing a portion of the uniform. But, "the bonds that hold band kids together is one of those ineffable things that is hard to describe to someone who hasn't experienced it."[1] And the joy of being a part of making beautiful music together is thrilling. It has been observed, also, that kids in the band do better on standardized tests than those who aren't. Also, my friend a choir teacher, told me she has trouble recruiting choir members because of the proliferation of electives.

An eighth grader in Blackhawk Middle School in Ft. Wayne, Indiana was given an assignment by his Spanish teacher. The students were to take a current event in the news and translate it into Spanish. This boy translated a Fox News story about US Navy Pilots who spotted an unidentified flying object. The teacher didn't like the source, informed him of that in front of the class, and said they were not to use Fox News for an assignment since it was "Fake News." She then instructed the boy to do a paper on "President Trump's Lies."[2]

A lady who is a teacher in the Denver Metro area told me of an experience regarding food in an elementary school cafeteria where she taught. In 2010 The First Lady implemented a program called the "School Lunch Initiative" ($5M). It was mandated by our federal government that the school lunches had to include two items. Even if the students didn't buy them in the cafeteria, they were to be given to them to increase their

nutrition. One was an apple, and the other was a carton of milk. As students checked out and paid, these items were put on their trays. There was a big trash can nearby and they walked right over and put them in the trash. I heard the identical story from a friend who volunteered at an elementary school near Colorado Springs. She was the volunteer assigned to put the "gifts" on the trays. Very few kept the gifts.

PART II

CHAPTER 3

In What Ways Has School Changed?

I have already related many changes, but there are more that should be mentioned. Schooling has ever been the laboratory for experimentation. Everything is fair game. Here are some examples.

Structure of the daily schedule--

Many schools now hold their classes for 90 minutes (2 traditional class lengths of time), and many schools have varied class lengths. Some do the 90 minute periods on Monday, Tuesday, Thursday, and Friday, with Wednesday having the regular 45 or 50 minute classes. In my view this keeps kids off-balance. Also, in regards to the classroom lessons to be taught—most of the "lessons" are gauged for roughly a 45 or 50 minute period of time. I haven't experienced two lessons being assigned, so usually after about 50 minutes the students have nothing to do, and spend the time with their cell phones. The 90 minute schedule is called block scheduling. Each day has half the schedule (maybe 1st, 3rd, 5th, and 7th classes), and the next day has the other half. I noticed students have a hard time concentrating on one course for 90 minutes. In the traditional setting, the lesson is presented and

students get some time to work on it (and are able to ask questions of the teacher), and the remainder becomes homework.

In some schools the day begins for students with "Seminar." It's usually from 7:30 a.m. to 9:00 a.m. The students usually just sit around and talk and play with their phones or sleep. If they want, they can sign out and go to another classroom for help. Many say they wish they could just stay at home and sleep.

Some schools have a rotating schedule. The first day the teacher teaches periods 1,2,3,4,5,6,and 7 (for instance). The next day he/she teaches periods 2,3,4,5,6,7,and 1, and so on. (This is tricky for subs since you may not be exactly sure what work is given to which class if the work differs from class to class.)

Cell Phones

On the subject of cell phones, you probably know all students have them. Students only reluctantly put them away in class. Einstein had a marvelous quote: "I fear the day that technology will surpass our human interaction. The world will have a generation of idiots."

The cell phone is such a pervasive technology that we all are in awe of it. It can be a tremendous boon to mankind, or it can be the opposite. There are some schools around the country that are banning technology because children are losing their ability to communicate face to face. A new book about that is *Disconnected*. Parents say they want to be able to communicate with their student at all times and that is the reason they buy students a smartphone. But wouldn't a "Dumb Phone" work as well—just to make calls. More on that in a later chapter.

Personal Classrooms Getting Rare

Many high school teachers don't have their own rooms now. Some are obliged to "travel." One teacher had a different room each period. She had to carry a backpack just like the students, and couldn't even spare a minute after class to answer a student's question. They are literally on the run. This makes it difficult for teachers. In many high schools, teachers have a work room where their "real" desk is. The desks in the classrooms are usually derelict desks.

Content

There have been content changes in the subject matter. Our history classes have changed, perhaps, the most. The magnificent stories of our nation's past are no longer being taught. The following will be a small example of what we have been deprived of knowing. We're taking a slight side journey into what an American history book used to contain. I found out about this from a beautiful contemporary book by Dr. Ben Carson entitled *America the Beautiful*. This story I'm about to relate was in our history textbooks until 1934 and then removed. It's about George Washington:

In 1755, during the French and Indian War, and way before the colonies wanted to separate from England, General Braddock, a famous English General, put together a contingent of British and Colonial soldiers to capture Fort Duquesne (also called Monongahela). Fort Duquesne was a French fort located about where Pittsburg, Pennsylvania is today. He put together quite a force for that day—about 1000 men—both British Regulars and militia from the colonies, mainly Virginia. George

Washington was 23 years old and a colonel in the Virginia Militia. (By the way, the Indians always sided with the French.) As they marched west toward the Fort, and as they approached it, they were ambushed by the French and Indians. The British were totally surprised and perfect targets for the bullets of the enemy. Nearly everybody died (including General Braddock—thus the battle is called "Braddock's Defeat"—the worst defeat in the annals of English arms to that time.) Only 23 officers survived, and all were wounded, except one—George Washington. Accounts say he had a bullet through his hat, four through his jacket, and two horses shot from under him. It was considered a miracle, and the subject of much discussion later back in Virginia. It was the subject of sermons and thanks to God. The Indians were extremely good shots and tried, under the direction of their chief, to "Kill the big one." (George Washington was 6'2".) Their bullets missed. A young girl, Mary Draper, who had been dragged off Draper Meadow, the family farm, and who had been with the Shawnee for some time, tells the story of some Frenchmen who had been at the battle, coming to the camp of the Shawnee. She understood their conversation since she spoke French. They were talking about George Washington. She had met Washington, so she listened carefully. They talked about shooting directly at him, but the bullets didn't seem to hit him.

Fifteen years later George Washington and Dr. Craig and a party of men were headed west to look at some land, and while they were in camp an old Indian chief and his braves approached. He was a Shawnee chief who had been at the famous battle. He said by way of an interpreter, and it was recorded at the time:

"I am a chief, and the ruler over many tribes...I have traveled a long weary path, that I might see the young warrior of the great battle. It was on the day when the white man's blood, mixed with the streams of our forest that I first beheld this chief. I called my young men and said, mark yon tall and daring warrior? He is not of the red-coat tribe—he hath an Indian's wisdom, and his warriors fight as we do—himself alone is exposed. Quick, let your aim be certain, and he dies. Our rifles were leveled, rifles which, but for him, knew not how to miss— 'twas all in vain, a power mightier far than we, shielded him from harm. He cannot die in battle. I am old, and soon shall be gathered to the great council-fire of my fathers, in the land of the shades, but ere I go, there is something bids me speak, in the voice of prophecy. Listen! The Great Spirit protects that man, and guides his destinies—he will become the chief of nations, and a people yet unborn will hail him as the founder of a mighty empire!"[1]

There are many such eerie and remarkable stories in our country's past, but none are included in our curriculum. In fact, I see patriotism played down, or simply not discussed at all. These stories foster patriotism. We cannot sustain our republic without patriots.

Making School Fun

Some more of the tinkering I see is a general change in school life to make school more palatable. There are "special days." The schools may do this to make school seem friendlier. Formerly, there were special days, but they were rare—maybe around graduation time. Schools now have a steady stream of special days. There are

Pajama Days. Both faculty and students wear their pajamas to school. Between gawking at each other and commenting or laughing at each other, not much work gets done. There are Red, White, and Blue days. Some students painted their faces white. Again, not a lot gets done since it is a special day. Then, there's "Hat Day." This seems like it might be easily controlled, but students are creative. One student I supposed was a girl because the hat he had on had a lovely veil, turned out to be a boy. Some wore stocking caps pulled down over their eyes! School work on those days was hindered. It seemed the administration had a never-ending source of ideas about how to make school more fun; sort of like a party.

Students were allowed to wear their Halloween costumes to school in one of the schools where I taught. They also had a contest for the school-wide best costume. The prize was to be given in the auditorium the last period of the day. Those who were in contention for best costume had to go to the auditorium to model their costumes one last time for the judges before the prize was given. The costumes the students came up with that day were amazing. One boy was Dracula. His costume was all black and he was on stilts. He said he'd fallen several times that day before I saw him. Another student was a swimmer with a very large float ring. She couldn't get through the door without taking it off which held up other students. The students who made it to the finals missed most of last period (when the judges had to look at them again) and would have to make up the work.

Anything different about the school building or classrooms these days?

The school buildings look pretty much the same. It takes a little period of time looking around to see changes. The thing that is obvious is that posted frequently around the building (for instance outside the boys and girls restrooms) are signs that say **SAFE ZONE**. (There is no teacher stationed inside the restrooms to prevent something untoward from happening.) Some teachers have these signs posted in their rooms as well. That gives a person pause. Does that mean that the areas where those signs are not posted are unsafe zones? Why does that need to be posted? Other interesting signage is about bullying. There are signs posted that say **NO BULLYING**, and one middle school even posted hand-made signs that said **NO BOY ON GIRL BULLYING** and **NO GIRL ON BOY BULLYING**! Also, there were the **DAY WITHOUT HATE** posters.

Games are played regarding bullying. When I was at one middle school we were given the rules for the scenario we were to follow during the last period. There were two circles of students: an inside circle and an outside circle. A student volunteers to be in the middle of the two circles. He or she states a made-up bullying scenario and one from the inner circle tells how it could be handled. That person goes to the center, and the center person goes to the outside circle. After we played the game I asked the students if there was a big problem with bullying at their school, and they said NO. I asked if any of them had ever been bullied and they said NO. This whole exercise was fun and a game to them, but not serious. There is an employee at that school who creates these

activities and distributes the papers with the rules and all the details of this session every week. It was very good to hear that these particular students didn't feel bullied.

More on Bullying

There is real bullying, however. We have always had bullying. A tragic case happened the fall of 2017 in Evergreen, Colorado. Students were at a before-the-start-of-school party. A boy was there who was being ridiculed terribly—so much so, that he went and threw himself off a bridge on Evergreen Parkway, and died.

I think the lesson here is that we must teach our kids how to handle this kind of awful treatment. First they must know when and how to extricate themselves from bad situations where there is obvious ill will. They need to know not to believe what others say, but to have a good enough self-image to reject those lies and insults. But they also need to know how to stand up for themselves, if need be.

I love the movie *The Bells of St. Mary's* with Ingrid Bergman and Bing Crosby. She's a nun in a boarding school, and she goes and buys a book on boxing and teaches one of her students how to box so he can defend himself against the playground bully. He fights him and wins the respect of the bully. He didn't run and tell the teacher he was being bullied. (It's reminiscent of the old adage: When seconds count, the police are only minutes away.)

There is cyber bullying too, which will come up later. Students these days are told to report bullying to their teachers, but not to do anything themselves by way of standing up to the bully. I think it is the preferred tactic—

not to confront the bully head-on. Kids, in my opinion, can be coached by parents about what to do. In most cases, though, students need to know how to handle these aggressive people themselves. When people become adults they will encounter bullying in life—at work and other places. There's no place to go to report it. There is bullying in adulthood! We have to learn how to stand up for ourselves—and we need to practice when we're younger.

Aspect of the classroom

One of the interesting things I noticed was the presence of a coffee pot in nearly every senior high classroom—along with a mini refrigerator and a microwave. In one classroom there were a lot of dirty coffee cups on the counter. I counted 42 of them. Many of the rooms were very messy with books and papers all over. Bookshelves were jumbles of books.

Adorned Classrooms

Another obvious change is the adorned classroom. I saw these especially in middle schools. Entering the classroom, one is aware of an overload of sensory stimulation. In some of the classrooms every inch of the wall seems to be decorated. Even the white boards have posters stuck to them. It is so much that the eye doesn't know where to look. There are pictures—framed and not framed, student art work, and just miscellaneous pictures covering the walls. This over stimulation detracts from the focus of the lesson since none of the decorations are lesson-related.

Teacher's Desk

In some classrooms, there is an actual teacher's desk— usually in the corner. Oftentimes the teacher's corner is completely decorated with personal information about themselves. There are pictures of their spouses, their kids, their car, their dog or cat, the pennant of the college they attended, maybe even a picture of the college, their favorite rock star, some sport figures they admire, and jerseys from the sport, and maybe some large or small stuffed animals in that corner. Often, however, there was no pencil or pen to use in the desk.

Absence of Books

The biggest difference in today's classroom that I see, is the absence of books. Seldom did I have a classroom where books were checked out to the students. The one memorable class where the students did have textbooks checked out to them (as I've mentioned before) was the calculus class at one of the high schools.

Homework

You may be wondering about homework, since there seem to be no books to take home. I believe some of the books (maybe all) are online and they can access them through the school website called Schoology. More frequently there is no homework. Students finish in class.

Desk Arrangement

Desks in rows are nearly a thing of the past. Students are almost always in groups of four. Assignments are often group assignments. Because of the differences in students (their work ethic, eagerness, and also ability) the effort to complete a project usually isn't spread

evenly among the members. Since normally the group gets one grade, there are understandably those who don't feel the need to work as hard. Often the teacher doesn't know who put in the most effort. There isn't individual work and individual responsibility as there is with single assignments given to students working on their own. Also, all schools have mainstreaming (students with disabilities are mixed in with the regular classroom), and many students don't want to partner with the slower kids.

I was happy to see chairs in rows when I walked into one high school classroom. However, as soon as the assignment was given the students began to move around so as to work with their friends. Desks were moving and the whole room looked like a cyclone had hit it. The students said their teacher allowed them to move around like that. At the end of the period, the students put the desks back in rows. Some of the students didn't go looking around at others' work, but sat quietly and did it all themselves. Those students finished the assignment faster than the others. It was better work as well as being more quickly done.

New things taught today

In one school there were posters all over: "We Love Our Earth." And they observe Earth Day. If the students were actually learning facts about earth, it would be time better spent.

One of the new things students are studying is the environment, and another is Sex Ed.—the latter starting in 4th grade. These are certainly new to the curriculum.

The most recent addition to the curriculum (2018) is that the Colorado State Board of Education has decided to teach 4th graders about guns. I wonder if they intend to teach them the importance of the 2nd Amendment

The very latest addition to the curriculum K through 12, was discussed on the *Tucker Carlson Show* 6/19/18 by Cathy Areu. The new subject is "toxic masculinity." She said boys are the violent ones in society, and this teaching is to curb that. She called it DDT (the pesticide) in boys, and that the future will be a matriarchal society. This concept of toxic masculinity is already taught in colleges.

Foreign Language Department

Another new term is the new designation for Foreign Language. The old "Foreign Language Department" has been renamed. It is now the "World Language Department." Words have meaning. It is the deemphasizing of nationalism in favor of globalism—the one-world approach.

Using Boxed Games at School

In one high school science class, the students were doing circuitry with a boxed game designed to demonstrate parallel and series circuits. But it is a game made for playing at home for students interested in electricity. The classroom should have books that teach the subject thoroughly and have lab experiments and lab books for learning it "hands on." Books and an over-all plan for teaching a subject were missing.

Biology Class Debate

In a biology class there was a debate—that's right, a debate! They were going to be signing up for a topic and then work to get ready for it. One of the topics was, "Are genetically modified foods good for society?" It was very straight-forward and the students understood what they were to do. The other topic caused lots of consternation: "Is stem cell research wrong?" The teacher really needed to give the wording of that one a second thought. (It would have been so much easier if the wording had been, "Is stem cell research beneficial?") It was hard to figure out who was Pro and who was Con! There is an immense amount of information to be transmitted in biology class—textbook work and lab work. Probably not a good idea to take a week out to have a debate when the pros and cons of both questions can be explained by the teacher in a portion of a class period.

Math Courses

I ran across students in math courses who didn't know which math course they were taking since there was no book. They didn't know if they were taking trigonometry or geometry or second year algebra. I wonder if they even knew the course title when they enrolled. Maybe it didn't have a typical course title since it was Common Core, and those courses have untraditional names.

A Language Change

I didn't once hear the term "TEST" in my subbing assignments. The new term is "assessments." The change of that word tends to make the event much less threatening and more palatable.

A Teacher's Day

You may wonder what a teacher's day is like. In high school, some teachers don't teach very many hours. Some department head teachers only teach around three hours—two one-and-a-half-hour classes. They may have a study hall and maybe a "home room" in addition. They have a planning period also where they can grade papers or make lesson plans. There are some teachers who teach more, but teaching 5 or 6 classes a day, each with 30 to 40 students, as it used to be, doesn't seem to be the case.

More New Things Students Are Being Taught That We Didn't Have Taught To Us

In the Fall of 2017, a New York 7th grade public school teacher passed out a flyer of a "genderbread" person (shaped like a gingerbread man cookie) that explained about genders. She also brought in a speaker for a 7th and 10th grade audience. The speaker gave the students a four-page handout with definitions of the following: homophobia, intersex, polyamory, pan sexual, bisexual, and cisgender topics. Do we wonder why the school day is having trouble fitting in the teaching of reading, writing, arithmetic, history, science, foreign language, band, choir, P.E., art, etc.?[2] A quote from a wonderful book is appropriate here: "One of the real shortcomings of a progressive education is the de-emphasizing of basic skills."[3]

Orange County, California

This is the newest bulletin out of Orange County, California. Parents in Orange County, California, may not opt their children out of lessons related to gender identity or sexual orientation, according to a memorandum by the school district's general counsel. I'll quote it: "Parents who disagree with the instructional materials related to gender, gender identity, gender expression and sexual orientation may not excuse their children from this instruction," reads the memorandum from the Orange County Board of Education.[4]

The Constitution and love for our country aren't taught

An alarming trend is that the U.S. Constitution often is not taught. High schools have a government/econ Class in the 12th grade. In government, the students learn about the federal government and about its three branches, and that their state sends two senators and also some representatives to Congress depending on the size of the state.

They aren't learning anything at all about their state. Actually that class would be termed "Civics." That has been dropped from most curricula. Ask your student if he/she knows the state representative for the neighborhood where you live—and the senator. Who's the Governor? How many counties does Colorado have? Why is Colorado called the Centennial State? If it's not taught, it's not learned, and there is so much to know.

Once, my son and I were invited to an event where Colorado legislators were the guests. My son was in college at the time. We were introduced to a large number of senators and representatives. As we were

driving back home he said: "Those couldn't all have been senators could they? We only get two." I said that they were *state senators*. He said: "Oh, does the state get senators?" I was shocked!

Some middle schools and high schools have dropped the Pledge of Allegiance at the start of the day. Some American flags have disappeared from classrooms. One reason our country is exceptional is that we have the only form of government designed to protect the people from the government. If students don't know the price that has been paid for this country, they won't feel the need to defend it.

National Anthem

In Ames, Iowa, a high school marching band had more than a dozen band members walk off the football field at a Friday night game while playing the National Anthem. More refused to play their instruments. This was in the fall semester of the 2017-2018 school year.[5]

The student leadership group at California High School in San Ramon, California, has banned the National Anthem at pep rallies. They state the third verse is racist.[6]

A Declaration of Faith

And this is taken from a newsletter from Michael Reagan. At a school in Virginia "a mandatory assignment had students practice calligraphy by copying the Muslim declaration of faith, 'There is no God but Allah.'"[7]

Mainstreaming

As I have mentioned earlier, there is "Mainstreaming." This is putting children with a disability in regular classes,

whereas in previous years these students were taught in special classes. (Mainstreaming became law in 1975 when the Congress passed PL94-142.) If the disability is mental, these students often look just like everybody else, but can't comprehend ideas quite as quickly—and sometimes not at all. They are often recognized by their behavior—and that doesn't take long. These are students who don't have outwardly noticeable disabilities. Mainstreaming also includes those with profound physical disabilities. A friend of mine in another state taught first grade and several years back commented she couldn't wait to retire. Her classroom had totally changed. She had a child with autism who ate the crayons.

Another teacher friend, also from another state, an art teacher in a high school, had a fellow who had two attendants to help him. The class one day was working with clay and forming clay pottery. This young man had the ball of clay given to him to work with. The two men who were attending him helped him roll the ball of clay around in his hands. The young man, however, was looking off in various directions.

Another one of his students was deaf. They were making jewelry. The boy accidentally dropped the stone he was working with. Because he couldn't hear, he didn't know where it dropped. He was so upset he picked up a hammer and threw it across the room.

I have never seen that in my subbing in Colorado, but I saw many classrooms impacted by Special Ed students who just didn't understand the assignment despite the fact that they had, sitting next to them, a helper trying to explain the work. They would often make odd sounds which disrupted the class. Students may be mainstreamed

who have physical disabilities, mental disabilities, and behavioral disabilities. Some of these disabilities are profound and they require an aide to be with the student continually. Even with that help, it is something for the classroom teacher to consider.

Often the pace of the whole classroom is slowed. Of course these students need to have access to education, but the setting and method are what should be considered. I was assigned to help a boy in a middle school math class with the regular teacher present and teaching. He couldn't answer the simplest questions asked, nor could he follow what she was showing on the board. He had entirely tuned out. He was beyond breaking down and crying. Because of distractions, the teacher had to teach in a very militant manner to keep the class together and going forward. Several of the students were similar to this fellow.

Mainstreaming of Immigrants

Mainstreaming is not always with children with physical/mental disabilities. One middle school student from Vietnam who hardly spoke English, was placed in a regular English class. He was being asked to analyze poems: looking for similes, onomatopoeia, metaphors, and alliteration. This young fellow literally imploded. He put his head down on his desk. The room was loud and disrupted. The teacher was in the room directing the activity and I was her helper. She assigned me to this young fellow, but my help and explanations were useless. He could hardly hear me for the class noise.

Change in parents' attitudes

There was a school in Jefferson County that wished to do something about the attire of its female students. Before this, the rule (not written) had been very simple—no belly buttons and no spaghetti straps. A meeting was held one evening in the auditorium to reinstate the former guideline for proper school attire. Guess who objected? The mothers! The dress guideline recommendation didn't pass.

Change in School Culture

In some school districts, students are now graded on their activism, volunteerism, and commitment to community rather than their academic knowledge. I don't think that's too prominent in Jeffco, but in some states it is.

Part of the new culture includes new words in common use: Earth Day is one, bullying is one, Safe-Zones, diversity, socialization, social justice, micro aggression, multiculturalism, politically correct, climate change, rubric, diversity, white privilege, racist, algorithm. Words we used to hear are now rare, like citizenship, on your honor, character, responsibility, test, competition, race (meaning how fast you can go).

The students look a bit different also. Colored hair is very popular—pink, green, blue. There are piercings. One girl had a nose ring that had a center stone in it. There is a lot of makeup used. There is tattooing. If students have the time to attend to all of this, they may not be putting their schoolwork first.

The New Culture of Teaching

The philosophy of teaching is different from what it was 60 years ago. A newly-minted 4th grade teacher shared some insights on how she teaches. Today's philosophy about selecting reading material is to have 80% of the material they read drawn from the last 15 years, and 20% come from literature before that. But, unless you think that the best literature was written in the last 15 years, students are missing out on a lot of good literature.

The modus operandi of teaching in years past was a teacher standing in front of a class and presenting the new lesson. The students listened, and perhaps took notes.

The practice of most of today's newly minted teachers is different. The idea is to get the students to do the teaching. The teacher is like a guide or cheerleader. That sounds good on the surface, but the teacher is the best prepared and most knowledgeable person in the room, and I want my child to be listening to the teacher. These new teachers disdain the "old model" of teaching. They call it "the teacher standing in front of the class and barking at the students." (The actual name for this "old model" type of teaching is "direct instruction.")

When I was a full time teacher I taught a lot of physics, and sometimes I would work until midnight to perfect how I would present an idea. When this young lady who teaches 4th grade visited an option elementary school in the area, where the teacher stands in front of the class and teaches, she came away from it feeling it was retrograde—with the desks all in rows and the students looking forward at the teacher. When the ITBS (Iowa Test

of Basic Skills) was still given in Colorado, this same school, with the rows of desks, consistently scored highest in the county—and sometimes the state.

She probably didn't know that people were so eager to get their little ones into this school that they would stop there on the way home from the hospital to put their babies on the waiting list for kindergarten. (That's back when we had a waiting list—up to the mid 1990s.) It's a lottery now. At one time there were over 1300 students waiting for this school, which only accommodated about 550 students.

In a new book by Daisy Christodoulou, *Seven Myths About Education*, she names the seven myths currently held by education experts:

> Facts prevent understanding
> Teacher-led instruction is passive
> The twenty-first century fundamentally changes everything
> You can always look it up
> We should teach transferable skills
> Projects and activities are the best way to learn
> Teaching knowledge is indoctrination

I find a kinship with her since what she is observing is basically what I have seen. At first the one about teaching transferrable skills seemed not to fit, until I remembered that school isn't charged with teaching skills unless we are talking about wood shop, metal shop, auto mechanics, and perhaps typing, etc. (Those, of course, are skills, but well worth knowing.)

New Politically Correct Speech

A new fifth grade teacher at Canopy Oaks Elementary in Tallahassee, Florida, is asking students to use gender-neutral pronouns in the classroom. A math and science teacher sent a request home in a letter to parents stating: "My pronouns are: '#...#my pronouns are they, them, their instead of he, his, she, hers.' I know it takes some practice for it to feel natural," the letter reads, "but students catch on pretty quickly." The letter also asks that students use "MX.," (pronounced 'mix') when addressing the teacher.[8]

At Salk Elementary School in Mesa, AZ, a 4th grade teacher changed a word in the Declaration of Independence. The word "men" was changed to "humans."[9]

In Dyer County, Tennessee, a senior girl was suspended after breaking a class rule. She had said "bless you" after a classmate sneezed.[10]

More new things

There are many things schools are teaching our students that we didn't have taught to us. As mentioned earlier, they are taking time to teach sex education, and the naturalness of homosexuality. Schools also spend time teaching global warming, and climate change. Looked at with a critical eye, we notice that education is becoming highly political.

Eliciting Obscenity

At a Jeffco school a couple of years ago, the new 7th graders were gathered into an assembly by their guidance counselor and the lights were dimmed. The counselor

announced that this was to protect each person's privacy. He then instructed the girls and boys to shout out every obscene and dirty word that they knew. Anything goes, he said—be specific. Silence reigned at first. Then a boy shouted out "DARN." After a pause, another said, "HECK." Another said "RATS." Then the counselor said, "Okay Let's just move on," When a parent complained about this request for obscene words, the counselor said this exercise was designed to prevent bullying.

Another child I knew came home crying from another local middle school. The teacher had given each student a blank piece of paper and asked the class to write down all the dirty words they knew, including curse words. Being a sweet and somewhat sheltered child, the girl knew very few unacceptable words. Because she only wrote down two or three words, the teacher scolded her and said, "Get busy. You know more bad words than that." Although the girl's mother requested to see the paper for this assignment, the teacher had already collected and destroyed them. What is going on here?

Headphones to Allow Music While Doing Homework

Another new activity in some schools is for teachers to lend out headphones. I saw this in a middle school. This enables students to listen to music on their cell phones while doing their assignments.

Comportment of Teachers

We remember working with our daughter to rid her of the over usage of the word "like." It was in every sentence. I see teachers today speaking in the same manner. They talk like teenagers. And, sadly, I believe they think it makes them very cool in the eyes of the students. Also,

the attire of teachers has slipped considerably. Teachers used to dress as though they were going to an office, but now they dress very casually. It's hard to find a teacher who is not in jeans.

What to do With Bad Teachers

School districts engage in something called the dance of the lemons. (Some other states call it the turkey trot.) That is where schools pass around poor teachers. The National Education Association (NEA), and the American Federation of Teachers (AFT) have contracts that are so iron-clad with the school districts, that the districts very rarely are able to fire teachers. Jefferson County has not only the NEA and CEA (Colorado Education Association), but an additional layer of restrictions with JCEA (Jefferson County Education Association).

Kissing and Hugging

Also, there is the issue of the students kissing and hugging in the classrooms and in the halls. The regular teachers are not correcting the students. Maybe there is no school policy about this, but there should be. I saw it in many high schools—more in some than in others—which may reflect more on the principal of that school. Students often use profane language and teachers will not correct them.

Students Sitting at Their Desks

Do you remember how we sat in our desks at school? Usually our feet were flat on the floor and we were working diligently on something on our desk (or listening to the teacher). Today, students put their feet on the desks—even their legs. Some girls engaging in that

practice have on shorts and it is very distracting to the boys.

Homecoming Royalty

My neighbors related a story that happened around the start of the school year—2017. One of their granddaughters is a cheerleader for her high school, so they went to see her cheerlead. This was in the greater metro Denver area, not in Jeffco. It was the Homecoming game. They were sitting in the stands watching the fun and then the Royalty were introduced and brought to the field. Afterward the King and Queen came and sat in the stands near my friends. The King and the Queen were both boys—one with a crown on and the other with a tiara!

A German Exchange Student's Assessment of Our Neighborhood School

In 1980 a neighbor had an exchange student from Germany who came to my house on Tuesdays to give German lessons to my four-year old daughter. One day I asked her how she liked our neighborhood high school she attended. She said, "It's a joke." She was the age of a sophomore, but our high school had put her in all senior classes where she was making all "A"s.

Invocation at Graduation

Another tradition that is being challenged is prayer at graduation and on other occasions at school. Many of us received an email several years ago about "The Sneeze." This account of a sneeze at a graduation ceremony prompting a "God bless you!" response that got around a prohibition against an official benediction being made

part of the ceremony. It's based on a true story, and here are the facts. It happened on May 20, 2001 during the commencement exercises at Washington Community High School in Washington, Illinois.

With the help of the ACLU, the family of Natasha Appenheimer, that year's valedictorian, brought suit to prevent the inclusion of the invocation and benediction traditionally given at the school's commencement ceremony. The suit was decided in the favor of the Appenheimers when, three days before the ceremony, the court handed down a temporary injunction barring the inclusion of the prayers on the basis of its being deemed "school sponsored." People were angered by the decision which overturned a tradition of 80 years' standing. Before the ceremony, students organized a prayer vigil around the school's flagpole. As an act of protest Ryan Brown, a member of the graduating class who was scheduled to give a speech during the event worked it out with the class that when he faked a sneeze at the podium, they were to cry out "God bless you." The audience stood and applauded.[11]

Other Things Our Students Are Being Taught

High school students in Jefferson County, at their teacher's behest, have left school and protested on street corners against school board members that were unfavorable to the teacher's union and that some teachers didn't like. The School Board election in 2012 was the first time in many decades that the Union was unsuccessful in getting its candidates elected. The Union went into action right after the election of the three members (a majority of the five-member board) to have

them recalled. They were successful, and the three served only two years of their four-year term.

In early 2018, a teacher at Hampton Middle School in Henry County, Georgia, told his students to write letters to Congress to enact stricter gun control laws. One of the students was the son of a police officer who happened to ask his son about his homework that particular night. He told his son, "You are not going to do that assignment." The father made public the assignment.[12]

Environmentalism is taught this way: that the whales are endangered, that the spotted owl is endangered, that the preble meadow jumping mouse is endangered, that the polar bears are endangered, that the earth is getting too hot—and something needs to be done about it. And students are led by their teachers to write letters to Congress about all these issues. The teachers are using the students as political pawns. They should be teaching substance—facility with math, language, and writing. Some of these things may be true, but that's not the teachers' charge. Teachers are charged with teaching basics.

Summary

Another summation seems to be called for. It is a terrible thing to bring friends bad news, but there is a need to know. I see students being denied content. I see the absence of books, the disparagement of memorization, and lack of self-reliance and initiative that education affords. I see students who have given up expecting much out of school. I see too much intellectual languor. I see little curiosity. Minds can wither, and I see that, plus the students are being taught moral relativism. As for

self-respect, it can only be earned—not given. All people gain it through the realization that they know something of value or can do something of value. It follows like the wake of a boat.

Sitting in a pod of four, either four desks pushed together or at a table for four, promotes what I call "Group Think." America is not like that. Individual work is important. Education enlivens the mind. The child's mind needs to be presented with the great thoughts of the centuries, the great literature, and the great discoveries, the stories of great men and women, some of whom gave us our country. Learning can be thrilling. We are the beneficiaries of all the enlightenment throughout the ages. They also need to have explained to them the preciousness of our Constitution; the miracle of America's existence. Worse, there has been an attack on the notion of right and wrong. Without that students—and adults—are rudderless.

It will not take very long for our competitor nations (China and Russia), educating their youth on a more rigorous merit-based model than we use, for their youth to overtake our youth academically. Not to mention their superior work ethic

CHAPTER 4

Results of These Changes

Children are not as informed as they once were. Also, our children are not as "in shape" as they once were. Our kids of today don't do much in the way of exercise. A recent article in *The Wall Street Journal* should awaken us all. It was entitled "19 is the new 60." I'll quote just a bit: "When it comes to physical activity, 19 is the new 60. That's according to a study published in June, 2017, which examined data from 12,500 people who wore tracking devices for a week. 'Activity levels at the end of adolescence were alarmingly low,' said the study's senior author, Johns Hopkins Prf. Vadim Zipunnikov, 'and by age 19 they were comparable to 60-year-olds.'"[1]

Our children aren't as tough and resilient mentally and physically as they once were. The differences in the way today's youth are being raised really shows up when they get to college. The recent presidential election caused mass hysteria among the progressive students in colleges across the country. Colleges cancelled mid-terms, created safe spaces, crying rooms, and some had a group primal scream! These kids are rightly called Snow Flakes.

Not Fulfilling Requirements

Are kids getting away with not fulfilling all the high school's requirements? Lately, educators and policy makers have pointed to the country's rising rate of graduation. This implies America is fixing its problem. But we find that those numbers are artificially inflated because of dumbed down standards. Recently Tennessee announced that many of its graduates weren't fulfilling the number of requirements needed to receive their diplomas. It was announced that one-third of graduates in Tennessee high schools had not completed all the required course work for a high school diploma.[2] As you will see, this is repeated across the other 49 states.

The 2017 National Assessment of Educational Progress (NAEP)—also known as the nation's "report card"—has been released. It is alarming.

A bit over a third of our 12th graders tested proficient or better in reading, and only one fourth did so in math. Among black students the scores were much worse—in the teens and single digits respectively.

These scores are only a part of the bad news. Did you know the high school graduation rate is over 80 percent. A high school diploma implies that the student can read and compute as a 12th grade level. As you can see there is a high percentage of students wrongly classified as proficient.

Our educators have been boasting about tremendous graduation rates—but many of the diplomas don't represent academic achievement. This is dishonest.

These diplomas only certify the students were in attendance.

This fraud is going on at higher levels of education as well. Colleges have access to these statistics, yet they admit, according to the Bureau of Labor Statistics, about 70 percent of white high school graduates. (To simplify, I'm only taking that segment.) They know that many of these students are ill prepared to be successful at college. Therefore, these is a rather new phenomena in colleges— a proliferation of remedial classes. One study suggests that more than 40 percent of students who go to four-year colleges take at least one such class. The percentage is higher in community colleges. Colleges are also creating majors where little analytical prowess is needed. Such majors often include the term "studies," such as gender studies, ethnic studies, American studies. These are majors for the most ill-prepared students. College students take the SAT or ACT tests. When students are ranked by their test scores, the students planning to be teachers rank in the bottom one half to one third.

Colleges are admitting young people who have not mastered what formerly was considered a ninth-grade level of proficiency in writing, reading, and arithmetic. Even after they graduate from college they often aren't up to a 12th-grade level of proficiency.[3]

There was a recent scandal at the University of North Carolina. The 2004 to 2012 members of the football and basketball teams were assessed to read between 4th and 8th grade levels. A few were below the 3rd grade level.

This ended in the reading specialist, Mary Willingham, resigning. She said something to the effect that the school should be more concerned about academics than athletics.[4]

Many people are questioning the advisability of going to college. Richard Vedder, professor emeritus of economics at Ohio University, and the director for the Center for College Affordability and Productivity, said that in 2012 there were 15,000 janitors, 83,000 bartenders, about 35,000 taxi drivers, and 16,000 parking lot attendants with a college degree. An estimated one third of college graduates are performing work formerly done by high school graduates.[5]

The American public just needs to be aware that there is academic fraud at every level. Knowing that there is a problem is the first step toward fixing it.

This reminds me of a boy I had in a 9th grade physical science class in 1974. We will call him John. That particular book on physical science was heavy on lab work. There were lots of labs, and the kids loved them. John was doing well. The class was mostly labs and, I did lots of explaining at the board about the labs, and John had a great memory. It wasn't until I decided to have this class read through the next chapter out loud in class, that I discovered John had a very hard time reading. The students were taking a paragraph at a time to read. When I came to John he said he would rather not read. I cajoled him that it would be just fine. So he read a very short paragraph, and I could see why he didn't want to read in front of his classmates. He stumbled over every

other word. After school I went to the counselor's office to check on his history of testing in reading. He hadn't been tested since 2nd grade. The reading specialist in the building called him down to her office for evaluation. He read at about the 2nd grade level and his schedule had to be changed to accommodate a class period for reading instruction.

Suicide

Something else is happening in school foreign to most of our experiences, and it's very alarming and sad. I am reminded of a statistic I read about high school students in Idaho: that 7% of them have tried to commit suicide. This was from about 2009. Schools should be teaching students a lot of real information they see as useful, and that will leave them with the feeling that life is hugely worthwhile.

Also, there is a brand new book, *Lost Connections*, by Johann Hari. In it he relates that our country is having a surge in suicides, even though more drugs for depression are being prescribed. And he talks about the need for feeding the starving affections of people.

Prom

Many of us remember prom very fondly. It was so much fun. For a girl, being picked up by her date and taken to dinner where they might meet other school friends similarly dressed up, was like a beautiful dream. For the boy, he got to practice being a man—going to pick up his date, holding the door for her, as he had been taught by his parents, treating her to dinner, and, after the dance, returning her home at a reasonable hour. The girl, by the

way, got to practice letting her date hold the door for her, seat her at dinner, escort her into the dance, and then walk her to her door at the end of the evening. These are all practice exercises for making the transition to adulthood.

Let me tell you about how it is being done today. The scenario just mentioned is still followed by most young people, but it is becoming increasingly popular to go in groups—group date. A bunch of girls gets together and goes out to dinner, and a bunch of boys does the same. They meet up at the prom and dance, but afterwards they go back home as they started. At first, when I heard about that, I thought how creative—a way not to have to miss out on prom. The more I think of it, however, I see it in a different light—more as students getting stuck in adolescence. Postponing maturing. It takes away any pressure or responsibility to perform—socially or financially.

Teenage Mothers

Some schools cater to the pregnant or new teenage mother by having nurseries in the school. Occasionally they bring the baby to class and the academic atmosphere is vaporized. This used to be the case in a Jeffco high school where I subbed long ago. I'm not sure it still exists there, but it does definitely exist in school districts across the country.

CHAPTER 5

An Unexpected Danger—Cell Phones

There is a new problem that has totally blindsided us—*the smartphone*! We have known about alcohol's dangers for a long time. Drugs have been warned against for almost as long—but phones? The problem with "screen time" has totally surprised us. In his fascinating new book *Disconnected* by Thomas Kersting, he describes this unexpected danger. Parents should definitely read it. It is causing ADHD (attention deficit hyperactivity disorder) in high schoolers. Kids having ADHD are usually diagnosed by 3rd grade. This new type is called "Acquired ADHD," according to Dr. John Ratey, Clinical Professor of Psychiatry at Harvard Medical School. The Journal of Clinical Psychiatry said ADHD diagnoses went up 45% in the US from 2000 to 2010. With repeated stimuli, the neural circuits in the brain become excited, and, if other neural circuits are neglected, they will weaken. The brain does something called "pruning" to these unused circuits. The brain weeds out neural pathways. It shows up as children being more comfortable in cyber space than in the real world. They have trouble looking you in the eye and carrying on a meaningful conversation.

Since children's brains are still maturing, they are most susceptible. This screen time makes children emotionally fragile. It is hard for them to handle day to day bumps in the road. Gary Small, Professor of Psychiatry and director of the UCLA Longevity Center at the Semel Institute of Neuroscience and Human Behavior, discovered that with as little as one hour a day online, the activity pattern of children's brains changed dramatically. Internet addiction showed physical problems such as higher impulsivity, anxiety, and depression. It takes three hours per day of screen time to change the brain. Some kids get eight hours per day several days a week. Since many of us see ideas most clearly through illustrations, I will include a piece from Kersting's book.

> "I want you to imagine the life of a typical sixteen-year-old girl for a moment. Let's call her Sarah. Sarah's mom enters her room each morning to wake her for school because Sarah somehow slept through the buzz of her alarm clock, even though it woke up the neighbors. Sarah likely got little sleep the night before because she couldn't pull herself away from the endless group chat she was a part of. After her mom's third or fourth attempt to wake her, Sarah finally emerges from her deep sleep, yells at her mom, and reluctantly gets on her feet. Sarah's first instinct, before she has even realized she's awake, is to reach for her cell phone, which is on her nightstand within arm's reach. She proceeds to brush her teeth, change into her clothing, and eat breakfast as she catches up on the text messages and social media gossip left over from the night before. Finally Sarah's mother is able to hurry her into the car in an effort to prevent her from being

late to school. During the short commute, Sarah moves her thumbs vigorously across the screen of her smartphone, completely oblivious to the world around her, including her mom. By the time her mom has reached the drop-off point, Sarah has already sent and received dozens of text messages since the time she got out of bed. As Sarah exits the car and walks towards the entrance of her school, her head is down, her eyes are fixated on her smartphone, and her thumbs are texting away. She never said thank you or good-bye to her mom. She is too distracted."[1]

There is an interesting article that appeared in the week end edition of the *Wall Street Journal* (Jan. 13-14, 2018) on the front page entitled "Parents' Dilemma: When to Give the Children Smartphones." This is a quote, and the language isn't great: "'Who the hell would give a junior-high school child a gaming platform to walk through the world with...It feels a little like trying to teach your kid how to use cocaine, but in a balanced way.' These parents worried if they could shield their son from addictive videogames, pornography, bullying and predatory strangers.

"Children spend nearly nine hours a day tethered to screens large and small outside of school according to Common Sense Media, a nonprofit that promotes safe media use for children." The article followed that "the goal of Facebook Inc., Alphabet Inc., Google, Snap Inc. and others is to create a host of captivating experiences that keep users glued to their screens. The more screen time, the more revenue." The article goes on to tell of advice given by Deborah Heitner, speaking in the auditorium of

Palo Alto High School, in Palo Alto California, that trying to "micromanage use of devices can prompt children to become more deceptive, especially in the fast-shifting digital environment where young people often maintain the upper hand."

Many teachers say that the attention span of students has shrunk in the years that smartphone habits have grown. The *Wall Street Journal* article goes on— "Parents say the apps. can enable them to locate their children instantly, but they also make it easy to keep parents at bay. Children set up Instagram accounts under pseudonyms that friends but not parents recognize. Some teens keep several of these so-called Finsta accounts without their parents knowing. An app. called Secret Calculator looks and works like an iPhone calculator, but it can double as a private vault to hide files, photos, and videos. For math homework, a student can point an iPhone camera at an algebra problem and Photomath will solve it. ...

"About 16% of the nation's high school students were bullied on line in 2015 according to the U.S. Centers for Disease Control and Prevention. Children who are cyberbullied are three times more likely to commit suicide according to the study in JAMA Pediatrics in 2014." Some mothers said in the article I've just quoted from, "that this piece of technology is like oxygen to their son or daughter. One man said, when considering when to buy his son a smartphone, that you have to decide at what age you are comfortable with him viewing pornography."

In a *Wall Street Journal* article of January 2, 2016 entitled: "Teach Your Children Well: Unhook Them from Technology," it talks about Waldorf schools. At Mountain Oak Charter School in Arizona, inspired by the Waldorf

schools, teachers say they can immediately detect who has been using devices at home.

Perhaps we should all take a cue from our technology giants regarding the school choices for their own children:

"LOS ALTOS, Calif. — The chief technology officer of eBay sends his children to a nine-classroom school here. So do employees of Silicon Valley giants like Google, Apple, Yahoo and Hewlett-Packard. But the school's chief teaching tools are anything but high-tech: pens and paper, knitting needles and, occasionally, mud. Not a computer to be found. No screens at all. They are not allowed in the classroom, and the school even frowns on their use at home.

"Schools nationwide have rushed to supply their classrooms with computers and many policy makers say it is foolish to do otherwise. But the contrarian point of view can be found at the epicenter of the tech economy, where some parents and educators have a message: computers and schools don't mix."[2]

Back in earlier times, when TV was the only screen vying for children's time and attention, I heard an amazing quote by a psychologist who had a radio show in the Denver market in the 1980s, Andrea VanSteenhouse. She said "Watching TV takes less energy than doing nothing." It has stayed with me all these years.

CHAPTER 6

Testing

Formerly the ITBS (Iowa Test of Basic Skills) was used as the standard in Jefferson County Schools. The reason it was a good test is that it was given across the nation—the same test. It was "tried and true." It had been used for many decades and was considered reliable by the school districts. The biggest thing, however, was that a parent could compare how his child and his child's school did compared to New York, Alabama, Washington, California, etc. You knew how everything stood nationally. Also, more importantly, a parent could tell how his child's school compared to the others in the district and in the state.

Jefferson County got rid of ITBS and replaced it in 1997 with C-SAP (Colorado Student Assessment Program). It came in under legislation in 1993. It's given at 3rd, 8th, and 11th grades. I've included two graphs of C-SAP scores which show a downward trend after 3rd grade. This is a test which tells if a student is working at grade level or below or above. No way is provided to compare how your student is doing compared to another in the same

system, or how a given school in general is doing compared to others in the District or State.

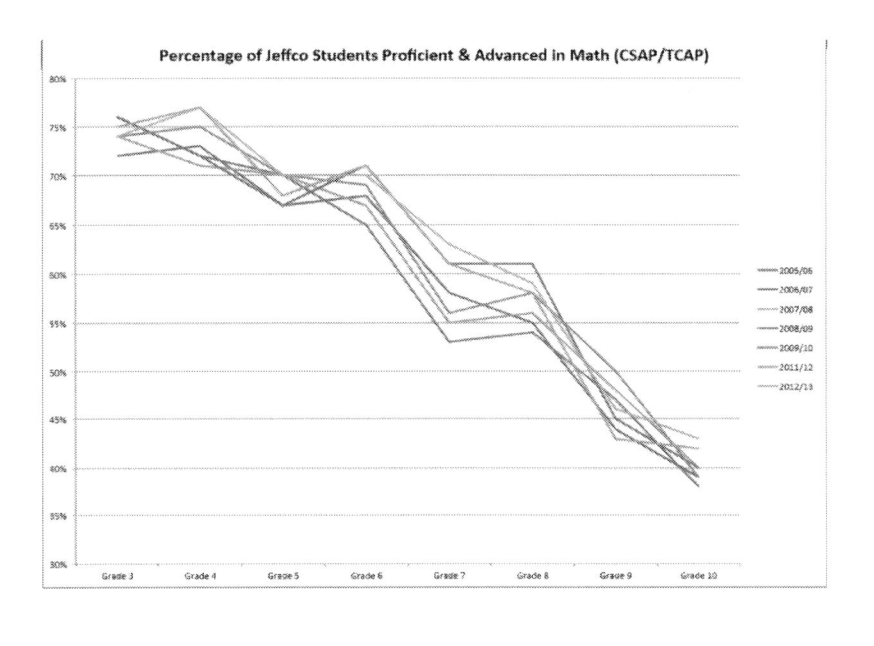

Percentage of Jeffco Students Proficient & Advanced in Math (CSAP/TCAP)

Math	2005/06	2006/07	2007/08	2008/09	2009/10	2010/11	2011/12	2012/13	2013/14
Grade 3	76%	72%	74%	76%	74%	76%	75%	74%	-
Grade 4	72%	73%	71%	72%	75%	75%	77%	77%	-
Grade 5	70%	67%	70%	67%	70%	71%	68%	70%	-
Grade 6	65%	68%	67%	71%	69%	71%	71%	70%	-
Grade 7	53%	58%	55%	61%	56%	61%	61%	63%	-
Grade 8	54%	55%	56%	61%	58%	59%	58%	59%	-
Grade 9	47%	44%	48%	45%	50%	47%	43%	46%	-
Grade 10	38%	39%	40%	40%	39%	42%	42%	43%	-
Grade 11 ACT Math & Science	-	-	-	-	-	-	-	-	42%

The C-SAP has given way to the Common Core PARCC testing—which neither the teachers nor the students can

see before or after the test. The students can't even get old tests to help study. Of course, in the 11th and 12th grades students typically take the SAT or ACT.

I understand, however, that Colorado is backing away from PARCC English and math tests as are many other states as they abandon Common Core. Are the tests we have chosen to give intended to hide how poorly we are teaching the children?

Just to remind you of all the iterations of schemes for modernizing and changing the schools' focus, here they are:

World Core Curriculum
America 2000
Goals 2000
Outcome Based Education
No Child Left Behind
Race To The Top (RTTT)
Common Core

Since these started, in the 1970s, there has been a decline in education proficiency. All of the above programs proceeded from influence of the United Nations. As you know, the federal government got into the business of education back in the late 1970s by creating the Department of Education. It is unconstitutional since the education of children is delegated to the states. The Department of Education was signed into law in October of 1979 by Jimmy Carter. It now takes about 4,000 people to run it, and has an annual budget of $68 million. Ronald Reagan said he would shutter it, but that didn't happen.

Did you know the SAT standardized testing was recentered downward in April 1995 because the students who were testing were doing consistently less well? They raised all the scores by 100 points. They just increased the scores by fiat. (The original scoring system was established in 1941.)[1]

The College Board put into its 2015 revised test some very negative things about America—it suggests that America is an aggressively exploitative country, that it has a grasping elite that oppresses Native Americans, blacks, women, immigrants, workers, and children. It minimizes the importance of America's founding. A few other details were filtered in, but were subordinate to this rancor.[2]

The New AP (Advanced Placement) U.S. History Text

A forthcoming 2019 edition of the U.S. History textbook published by Pearson and intended for AP Classes has impressed many with its clearly leftish political bias. An excerpt from the updated textbook gives their opinion of the motives of those voting in the 2016 election.

> "Trump's supporters saw the vote as a victory for people who, like themselves, had been forgotten in a fast-changing America—a mostly older, often rural or suburban, and overwhelmingly white group. Clinton's supporters feared that the election had been determined by people who were afraid of a rapidly developing ethnic diversity of the country, discomfort with their candidate's gender, and nostalgia for an earlier time in the nation's history. They also worried about the mental stability of the President-elect and the

anger that he and his supporters brought to the nation. (This is a remarkable attempt to politicize history.)"[3]

Are we still adequately educating our kids? No! I would like here to show you a test generally given to 8th graders in 1895 upon completion of 8th grade—the highest grade most of our grandfathers and great grandfathers achieved. (At 13 they usually had to go to work to help support the family, so their education was terminated.)

" What it took to get an 8th grade education in 1895

--Remember when grandparents and great-grandparents stated that they only had an 8th grade education? Well, check this out. Could any of us have passed the 8th grade in 1895?
This is the eighth-grade final exam from 1895 in Salina, Kansas, USA. It was taken from the original document on file at the Smokey Valley Genealogical Society and Library in Salina, KS, and reprinted by the Salina Journal. We can be overjoyed it is not used today.
8th Grade Final Exam: Salina, KS -1895
Grammar (Time, one hour)
1. Give nine rules for the use of capital letters.
2. Name the parts of speech and define those that have no modifications.
3. Define verse, stanza and paragraph
4. What are the principal parts of a verb?
Give principal parts of "lie," "play," and "run."
5. Define case; Illustrate each case.
6 What is punctuation? Give rules for principal marks of punctuation.

7 - 10. Write a composition of about 150 words and show therein that you understand the practical use of the rules of grammar.

Arithmetic (Time, 1.25 hours)

1. Name and define the Fundamental Rules of Arithmetic.

2. A wagon box is 2 ft. deep, 10 feet long, and 3 ft. wide. How many bushels of wheat will it hold?

3. If a load of wheat weighs 3942 lbs., what is it worth at 50 cts/bushel, deducting 1050 lbs. for tare?

4. District No 33 has a valuation of $35,000. What is the necessary levy to carry on a school seven months at $50 per month, and have $104 for incidentals?

5. Find the cost of 6720 lbs. coal at $6.00 per ton.

6. Find the interest of $512.60 for 8 months and 18 days at 7 percent.

7. What is the cost of 40 boards 12 inches wide and 16 ft. long at $20 per meter?

8. Find bank discount on $300 for 90 days (no grace) at 10 percent.

9. What is the cost of a square farm at $15 per acre, the distance of which is 640 rods?

10. Write a Bank Check, a Promissory Note, and a Receipt

U.S. History (Time, 45 minutes)

1. Give the epochs into which U.S. History is divided

2. Give an account of the discovery of America by Columbus.

3. Relate the causes and results of the Revolutionary War.

4. Show the territorial growth of the United States.

5. Tell what you can of the history of Kansas.

6. Describe three of the most prominent battles of the Rebellion.

7. Who were the following: Morse, Whitney, Fulton, Bell, Lincoln, Penn, and Howe?

8. Name events connected with the following dates: 1607, 1620, 1800, 1849, 1865.

Orthography (Time, one hour)   1. What is meant by the following: Alphabet, phonetic, orthography, etymology, syllabication

2. What are elementary sounds? How classified?

3. What are the following, and give examples of each: Trigraph, subvocals, diphthong, cognate letters, linguals

4. Give four substitutes for caret 'u.' 5. Give two rules for spelling words with final 'e.' Name two exceptions under each rule.

6. Give two uses of silent letters in spelling. Illustrate each.

7. Define the following prefixes and use in connection with a word: bi, dis, mis, pre, semi, post, non, inter, mono, sup.

8. Mark diacritically and divide into syllables the following, and name the sign that indicates the sound: card, ball, mercy, sir, odd, cell, rise, blood, fare, last.

9. Use the following correctly in sentences: cite, site, sight, fane, fain, feign, vane, vain, vein, raze, raise, rays.

10. Write 10 words frequently mispronounced and indicate pronunciation by use of diacritical marks and by syllabication.

Geography (Time, one hour)   1 What is climate? Upon what does climate depend?

2. How do you account for the extremes of

climate in Kansas?
3. Of what use are rivers? Of what use is the ocean?
4. Describe the mountains of North America
5. Name and describe the following: Monrovia, Odessa, Denver, Manitoba, Hecla, Yukon, St. Helena, Juan Fernandez, Aspinwall and Orinoco.
6. Name and locate the principal trade centers of the U.S.
7. Name all the republics of Europe and give the capital of each.
8. Why is the Atlantic Coast colder than the Pacific in the same latitude?
9. Describe the process by which the water of the ocean returns to the sources of rivers.
10. Describe the movements of the earth. Give the inclination of the earth."

"Notice that the exam took FIVE HOURS to complete. Gives the saying "he only had an 8th grade education" a whole new meaning, doesn't it?!"

This shows how poor our education system has become. I didn't have the answers, and I failed the 8th grade test.

That is why the home schoolers look for the oldest history texts and English anthologies and grammar books they can find. They are more accurate and the writing is of a higher standard.

As if this news about the 1800's test wasn't bad enough, here are the statistics on a world-wide test that was given

recently. "One of the biggest cross-national tests is the Programme for International Student Assessment (PISA), which every three years measures reading ability, math and science literacy and other key skills among 15-year-olds in dozens of developed and developing countries. The most recent PISA results, from 2015, placed the U.S. an unimpressive 38th out of 71 countries in math and 24th in science. Among the 35 members of the Organization for Economic Cooperation and Development, which sponsors the PISA initiative, the U.S. ranked 30th in math and 19th in science."[4] We are officially behind Estonia. In the 1950s the U.S. scored near the top.   Will western civilization, which is the noblest and mightiest mankind has ever seen, built on the heritage of Locke, Milton, Voltaire, etc. and all the brilliant Founding Fathers—with its wish for unfettered pursuit of Truth—be able to continue to exist?

Family Letter from the Civil War

We, my family, are fortunate to have in our files a letter from an ancestor from the 1800s. He was fighting in the Civil War at the time. I include it only to illustrate the level of thinking of the most common and standard of the people of that day—how elevated it actually was. This great great (and maybe another great) uncle was a teenager and had only an 8th grade education. It was a letter from the battle-front (Civil War) to his brother back home. Be looking for word usage and grammar.

Fort Donelson,
Monday, March 3, 1862

Dear Brother Charles,

I have just received your letter of the 23rd ultimo and it was read with great interest and I will hasten to answer to inform you that I am still around.

We have just had marching orders again. We are to cook three days rations and be ready to march at a moments warning; consequently I hav'nt much time to write. We do not know certainly where we are going, but it seems to be the openion that we are going on to Memphis; and it is very evident that we are going to have another big fight.

In regard to Mrs. Pettingers spirit-communication, it is all false. There is nothing in it. I am not under the doctors care nor have I been since I have been in the service, but on the contrary have been in my place in the ranks, every time the ranks have been formed, and no one can say that I ever flinched from duty. Although a great many on our company gave out during the fight, on account of the hardship and exposures they became sick and exhausted; and during the last two days of the fight not one half of our company could be mustered for duty.

But I am proud to say that I have been in the ranks every time and have seen the fight from beginning to end. If I am spared to return home I will then tell you all about it and I shall be able to tell you a story that will make you shudder. I have been on the battle field where I could

stand in my tracks and count over one hundred bodies within sight of me: and I have seen as many as sixty five bodies buried in one grave.

The siege of Fort Donelson is, in one sense the greatest battle that ever was fought on this continent. Nowhere in history do we read an account of so many prisoners being taken in any one battle.   Gen. Washington, when he captured Lord Cornwallis only took some ten thousand prisoners.   In this battle, we have taken just 17,770.   This is calculated to be the correct report.   But I can not stop to write much this time, as my time is too limited. We have had very fine weather here for several days until yesterday when it began to grow cold and today it is quite cold. I am very glad to hear that you are well and enjoying yourself so well.

I congratulate you in your happiness and hope that you may enjoy many happy rides and pleasant evenings in the society of friends there, and I cincerely hope that my life may be spared to meet you again before many days. But I will close my letter for this time, hoping that it may find you well and that you will answer it soon. Give my love to all enquiring friends and accept this from,

Your most affectionate brother,

Edward Sutton

I have accurately copied the letter above, mistakes and all.   Nevertheless, you can see what a fine job of communicating this is. I am not sure many of our young

ones could write a letter this straight forward and clear and informative, and, yes, brave.

I just came across this interesting quote: "Something strange has been going on in government schools, especially where the matter of reading is concerned. Abundant data exist to show that by 1840 the incidence of complex literacy in the United States was between 93 and 100 percent....Yet compulsory schooling existed nowhere."[5]

PART III

CHAPTER 7

Are Colleges Still As They Were?

Are things at the college level faring better? As I've indicated earlier, maybe not. Be careful about sending your children to college. There is silliness in colleges too. (Maybe "silliness" is putting it too kindly.)

There is a story out of Springfield College in Massachusetts that gets attention. An English professor, Dennis Gouws, proposed teaching a "Men in Literature" course and found it was one too many such courses (his was the only one), even though there are more than 900 women's studies programs and thousands of classes about women in literature in colleges today. On March 26, 2007, the college dean of Arts, Sciences, and Professional Studies, Anne Herzog, wrote a letter to Professor Gouws placing him on "Official Warning Status."

This isn't the first attack. He has had nearly two years of bullying. His problems regarding this course have spilled into almost everything else he has tried to do. He requested a sabbatical during which time he planned to finish a book that was under contract. He was denied. The syllabi for his other courses were questioned. He has had dozens of petty directives to which his colleagues

were not subjected. He has complied with the directives. However, he did ask why he was being asked to submit to these directives—and that they be put in writing. He asked if he could bring a witness to these meetings. He was denied both with no written explanations. Dean Herzog has taken the preliminary steps to fire Professor Gouws.[1] When I checked recently, Professor Gouws is still at the college.

A Trinity College professor, Johnny Eric Williams (Associate Professor of Sociology) calls white people "inhuman." He says "Let them f-ing die."[2]

Dartmouth has changed considerably. Did you know that you can graduate from Dartmouth with a degree in English without studying Shakespeare?

"WASHINGTON, DC—According to a new study, fewer and fewer of America's top colleges require English majors to take a course on William Shakespeare. The American Council of Trustees and Alumni is releasing the study in conjunction with Shakespeare's birthday on April 23 as the nation's capital continues a six-month celebration of his work.

"'The world loves Shakespeare,' ACTA president Anne D. Neal said. 'But American universities don't. That's what our study shows.'

"The study, *The Vanishing Shakespeare*, looks at English departments at 70 universities public, private, large and small, in all geographic regions. It finds that only 15 of them require their English majors to take a course on Shakespeare.

"A degree in English without Shakespeare is like an M.D. without a course in anatomy,' the report declares. 'It is tantamount to fraud.'

"It continues: 'A high school that hires someone with a B.A. in English should rightly assume that this individual can teach Shakespeare and other great authors. However, in a world where Shakespeare is no longer required, it's easy to imagine a day when school teachers will not have read Shakespeare, and will not teach him.'"[3]

The University of Pennsylvania replaced the image of Shakespeare in the English Department building with a photo of Audre Lorde, a black feminist poet. Shakespeare's portrait was removed to the English department chair's office and left there.[4]

The University of California Davis has listed some new pronouns. They are gender neutral. They were offered by the LGBTQIA community there. They are (and this is not a complete list) Zo/Zir/Zirs/Yo/Yas.[5] They have been exported to other universities such as Vanderbilt. You can google it at LGBRQIlifevanderbilt   To use another pronoun referring to a person who has designated that he/she wants to use these pronouns is considered a micro aggression.   This was featured on Fox News' *Tucker Carlson* show on April 3, 2018. The guest, Cathy Areu, explained it.   She mentioned that there are other universities adopting the new pronouns.

Canada has the same issues arising. Jordan Peterson, a Psychology Professor at the University of Toronto, has found himself at the center of this controversy. I'll quote from a book about him that I just finished reading. "I just sat in my bloody office at home and threw up a couple of

amateurish videos, more or less attempting to articulate my feelings about a couple of policies, and it's like all hell broke loose. And why? Well, because that hell is right underneath the surface." What he said that was so offensive, was that he planned to keep using the "binary" pronouns. In other words, the ones we use regularly—he, him, his, she, her, hers, etc. The school had just adopted the new gender neutral pronouns. It was actually in the process of becoming federal law in Canada. The bill was called Bill C-16. It had passed the House of Commons in October of 2016 with a vote of 248-40. As of January 2017, the bill still awaited senate hearings. I just learned it passed June 15, 2017.

Another quote that is significant from Peterson is the following: "There's a difference between saying that there's something that you can't say and saying there are things you *have* to say. I regard these made-up pronouns—all of them—as the neologisms of radical PC authoritarians." "I'm not going to be a mouthpiece for language that I detest, and that's that."[6] There will be punishments—presumably fines—for knowingly miss-speaking. The school called a rally where faculty, administration, and students attended. Only the students defended Peterson.

You remember the "Snowflakes" of November 2016 mentioned earlier? They are students who have to have exams cancelled and be put in a room where they can get hot chocolate, be given Play Dough and jelly beans and watch kitten movies and have puppies brought in. And our colleges are fostering that! Actually, from what I've seen, I don't know if our country could muster enough youth with integrity and backbone to fight today. How

can someone fight and defend something he doesn't believe in or value.

Edward Everett said: "Education is a better safeguard to liberty than a standing army." But students have to have that education. Our country is the envy of the world. Education is what we think our students are getting at school, but are they? Most people are aghast at the fragile sensitivities of the present students.

The Cry Closet at the University of Utah

That's right! The University of Utah had a Cry Closet. It was called: "A Safe Place for Stressed-Out Students; Otherwise known as 'The Cry Closet'." It had five rules posted on the door.

1. Knock before entering
2. Only one person in the closet at a time
3. Limit your time in the closet to no more than 10 minutes.
4. Turn lights and timer off before leaving
5. Use #cryclosetuofu if posting on social media

The page further says: "These rules must be followed seriously because the university may not want any funny business happening inside the closet meant for crying. It might be like common sense, but the rules are made to remind people to use proper manners while they're crying or about to cry." I've copied it exactly. This was a project of some students, not the school, and it was set up in the library for seven days during finals week.

Comfort Pets

Institutions have long made accommodations for service animals—such as seeing-eye dogs. They have, of course, stayed in dorm rooms with their owners. Now colleges are making accommodation for "comfort" animals (dogs and cats).

At Arizona State University a professor let students organize an anti-Trump rally instead of taking the final exam. Regardless of how one feels about President Trump, would you like your hard earned tuition dollars to be spent letting students miss the final—something they have worked toward all semester—the pinnacle of illustrating their mastery of the material?[7]

Many radical students are demanding that several Western classics be replaced because they are "outdated, Eurocentric" works. At Columbia University in New York, traditional works such as the poems of Ovid, Shakespeare's King Lear, The Odyssey, and Plato's "Symposium" are under attack, and students are demanding they be replaced with less Eurocentric reading assignments.[8]

At Yale University you can be kept from printing an F. Scott Fitzgerald quote on a shirt according to the *Wall Street Journal*.[9] Smith College doesn't like the n-word that appears in *The Adventures of Huckleberry Finn*. Their students are demanding the book be banned. This is an American classic. NewSouth Books announced it would publish a version of *The Adventures of Huckleberry Finn* with the "n-word" removed.[10]

One of our great military academies is in trouble. An email I received from a 1986 graduate of the Air Force

Academy, L. Todd Wood, entitled "The United States Air Force Academy Doesn't Train Warriors Anymore" confirmed what I knew has also been happening at higher levels of education. He returned to the Academy for his 30th reunion and this is what he saw. I'll quote him directly.

> "I realized something was horribly wrong when I arrived at the bottom of the ramp to the cadet area which used to say "Bring Me Men" above the tunnel entrance. It was an iconic quote, and we were taught at that time that "men" meant the human race, not necessarily only the male sex of such. I'll meet you at the bottom of the 'Bring Me Men' ramp was a routine line to girlfriends, boyfriends, parents, etc. who came to visit their cadet at the academy. I never heard any animosity against this quote during the four years of my stay at the Blue Zoo. Imagine my shock when I saw the quote had been changed to some PC gibberish about 'Integrity First. Service before Self. Excellence in All We Do.' Ten words! At first, I laughed at the thought of some cadet telling his civilian girlfriend to meet him at the bottom of the Integrity First. Service Before Self. Excellence in All We Do' ramp. But after a quick laugh, I felt sadness at the loss of tradition, and loss of basic masculinity of warfare being taught at the academy. It was then I knew it was gone. I also felt alarm—*if they changed this, what else have they changed? This can't be good for training the future Air Force warriors.*

"My next stop, the next horror, was walking around the cadet area with my fellow classmates from the Class of '86 and a few others. The place looked about the same...But there was something very, very wrong. I couldn't place it, but then it hit me. It was October. The fourth class cadets should not have been 'recognized' yet. That meant being accepted in the ranks of the upper class and the associated privileges that come with it. This entailed walking at attention, squaring corners, greeting upperclassmen, and other general military training. None of this was happening. They were walking at rest, not greeting anyone. Actually, they were ignoring the upperclassmen walking by. I stopped one of them and asked him, 'Cadet, are you recognized yet?' 'No, we are not' was his response. He kept walking. There was no 'sir' in his response. He obviously knew I was an alumnus and former military officer. The problem was that *he simply didn't care*. He didn't care because he had been taught not to care. Military bearing was absent. Completely gone. Removed. And the shock continued. As the time started to get close to the Noon Meal Formation, where the cadets form up and march into Mitchell Hall for lunch, I again realized nothing was happening. Cadets were nonchalantly walking to the huge cafeteria where they all met at once during the school week for lunch. I subsequently found out the formation had been cancelled due to high winds. I laughed to myself. There wasn't even a breeze. ...Inside the noon meal, all former military decorum and

98

training at the lunch table had been vaporized. There was nothing. The freshman cadets didn't even have the civilian decency to serve their alumni guests first, not to mention any military bearing. They just took the food and ignored everyone else at the table. It gets worse: after lunch, my colleagues walked into the academic building. Before my eyes, where there used to be formal lecture halls, was a Dunkin' Donuts. My jaw hit the floor and I actually took a picture—I was that amazed. This was no longer a military academy; it was UCLA in uniforms. We then visited the dorm rooms. We nonchalantly walked into one cadet's room who had the door open, which was the custom. We asked them a few questions. They didn't get up. They didn't greet us formally. They just sat there. These were fourth classmen. I guarantee you that in the past, if an alum had walked into a fourth class room the residents would be at attention within seconds and the 'sirs' would be flying like birds on a high wire."[11]

I'll end there. I quoted a lot to give the full flavor of the situation, since my readers may not have known. This was included with the permission of the author.

At UNC (University of Northern Colorado), the men's basketball team was stripped of its 2011 championship because it was learned that coaches took the academic tests for some players.[12]

The Vice Provost of New York University claims restricting speech on campus can be a "public good." Higher education is for the free interchange of ideas. Not to mention the 1st Amendment!

"Earlier this week, Ulrich Baer, a vice provost at New York University, published an op-ed in *The New York Times* defending student-activist efforts to shut down speakers at institutions of higher education like Auburn, UC Berkeley, and Middlebury."[13] Political correctness is a weapon used to silence unwanted speech.

Stanford no longer requires Western Civilization classes. Only 2% of colleges offer Western Civilization as a course requirement even for history majors.

Were you aware Marx's *Communist Manifesto* is the single most frequently assigned text in the college classroom other than the Strunk and White grammar manual? There are 4,120 self-declared Marxists (Communists) teaching sociology on U.S. campuses today.[14]

Fifty-three undergraduate history programs of the 76 highest ranked colleges don't require even a single American history course to fulfill the history major.[15]

February 13, 2018, Fox News covered a story out of Princeton. A university professor there—a Sociology Professor—had a seminar on Free Speech. He mentioned the "N" word—not directed at anyone, just as a word, and the whole class got up and walked out of his seminar. Some even shouted the "F" word at him.

Bret Weinstein, a popular long-standing professor at Evergreen State University outside of Seattle, has been forced to resign. His conflict with the school was that he believed it is okay to discuss religion, culture, and race from all perspectives—even white ones. His other infraction was that he refused to leave the campus grounds on a day the school had declared "no whites for

the day." He said, "I'm not going to leave because of the color of my skin." Also, he had been interviewed on a right-of-center program.[16]

Did you know that the University of Tennessee, Knoxville, just finished what has become a yearly event? It ran from April 6th to 12th , 2018. It's called "Sex Week." It boasts such offerings as: Butt Stuff, Masturbation Nation, Toys R Sex, Gender Smack down, The Science of Abortion, and a Drag Show. There are many other offerings. You can check them out on Google.

The *Washington Post* ran an article recently about how to be a rebel—it was to go on a date! Since rebellion started to be the fashion in the 1960s, it has been hard to be a rebel—since everyone had the same goal—to be different. A professor of philosophy at Boston College, Professor Cronin, found a way to encourage real rebellion. She challenged students to ask someone on a date—just a simple date. She included only two requirements: no alcohol and no physical contact. Professor Cronin said it's a "weirdly countercultural thing to do." Even parents are telling their students not to get caught up in a relationship—that they need to get their careers on track before thinking about that. Some parents advise their students just to "hook up" and move on. Sad that it has come to this—a twisted age.[17]

Graduations are no longer quite as we remember. I attended an out-of-state college commencement recently and was surprised to learn that it is now all right to decorate the mortarboard. More than half of them were adorned with writing, glitter, beads, glued-on silk flowers, and one even looked like it had small trees growing out of it. Many also wore leis—just for fun. The graduates, who

were seated on the floor of the field house waiting to walk across the stage, were tossing around a beach ball— just batting it around overhead. The graduates, of course, didn't toss their caps in the air!

The printed program listed the Ph.D. candidates along with their theses titles. Here are a few: "Discursive Constructions of Gender Through Dramatic Play: A Feminist Poststructural Analysis;" "An Exploratory Study of Female Representations in Exergames and Their Related Impacts on Adolescent Females;" and "Queer is the New Capitalism: Neoliberal Technologies and a Blueprint for the Left Beyond Identity Politics."

The MIT press has just published a new book entitled: *Communism for Kids* by Bini Adamczak, extolling the benefits of Communism. The very first sentence of this book says: "Communism names the society that gets rid of all the evils people suffer today in our society under capitalism."

Our students do not know that Communism in the 20th Century was responsible for the deaths of 130 million people—in peacetime—killed by their own governments. It's a moral scandal that people don't know about the 100 million murdered in the Soviet Union, and that Stalin starved 5 million Ukrainians in 1932-33. It was called the Red Famine.

The idea of Utopianism or "one for all and all for one" is tempting as a concept. There is just one thing that gets in the way—it goes against human nature! Did you know Communism (commune-ism) was tried in America? When the Pilgrims came to Massachusetts they lived under it for a year. If ever there was an advantageous set of

circumstances for it to work, that was it. These people loved each other, and they came over from England together. They were of the same religion, background, and customs. They pledged to work together for the good of the colony and everybody would profit equally from it. They nearly starved until William Bradford, their leader, declared during that second year that every man could have his own plot of ground to do with it as he wanted, and sell or trade from his enterprise as he chose. Under the old way, knowing that all would share alike, some men (and women) took their ease knowing they would still get an equal share. Bradford's change brought all hands out to work. They began to prosper. The women during the first experiment decided they didn't really like washing some other man's clothes. The men wanted to build shelters for their own families. They were no less friendly after this change, just more motivated to help their own families. We must learn the great fact that free men are not equal, and equal men are not free.

I just discovered that the new "word" among millennials is WOKE. I'm not sure what that means, but we might want to watch (listen) for it.

Before leaving this "College" topic, I would like to leave you with the names of at least two colleges that offer a standard rigorous curriculum similar to the 1950s and before. They are: Hillsdale College in Michigan, and Grove City College in Pennsylvania. Both take no government funds, and thus are free to choose their curriculum and books.

PART IV

CHAPTER 8

What Can We Do About The Changes We See As Detrimental ?

If you have students who are making "A"s and "B"s you may not think anything needs to be done. That may or may not be the case. Until you actually quiz them on what they know, you won't be able to tell if some change needs to happen. I thought of a few simple questions you can ask them to get a quick "feel" for their knowledge:

1. Who was the Marquis de La Fayette?
2. Who wrote Poor Richard's Almanac?
3. In which half of the 1800s did the Civil War occur?
4. What are the eight parts of speech?
5. Who was Winston Churchill?
6. Do a long division problem —say 364 into 9844 (leaving the remainder as a fraction that has been reduced).
7. Who said "I regret I have but one life to give for my country?"
8. How many times does the word "Democracy" appear in the Declaration of Independence and the Constitution?
9. Who wrote "A Penny Saved is a Penny Earned?"
10. Who said "Let them Eat Cake?"
11. In the classic book A Tale of Two Cities, what are the two cities?

12. Have them add 1/5 + 1/8.
13. What was Auschwitz?
14. Who was the first person to set foot on the moon?
15. What is a gerund?

Multiplication Tables Need to be Memorized

Lastly I want to relate a unique method a teacher devised for teaching the multiplication tables. This, of course, was years ago. This 6th grade teacher quizzed the students first thing in the morning while they were still fresh. She had written out a series of multiplication problems like 3 x 5, 4 x 8, etc. The class took out a piece of paper and they were to write down the answer to these products. She read them rapidly and so the students needed to have the answers so immediately in mind that it was a reflex action to write the answer. She had 20 or 30 questions. The students exchanged papers to grade them. The teacher did that every day until all the class got 100%. It took until February. The students lagging behind were helped by their fellow students so they could quit having that quiz every day. (By the way, Kumon math, which is common today, is loved by the students who use it because it gives them a similar reflex knowledge in converting fractions to decimals and percentages, among other things—a big leg up when students get to high school and are solving complicated problems.) The above described method would probably be frowned upon in today's educational setting since competition is discouraged, and memorization is also discouraged.

A Genius Way of Teaching Grammar

A teacher who had a great way to help students with their grammar, did this: one day of the week for a portion of

the class period she accepted examples of what the students brought in and thought were examples of poor grammar that they had seen in print or heard on the radio. (The radio was all they had in those days.) All week the students collected what they thought were specimens of incorrect grammar. They discussed the instances and learned the correct way, if there actually was a grammatical error. The students learned grammar rules very fast. They also did lots of diagramming sentences.

Vouchers

If vouchers ever make it to the ballot, please vote for them. A friend of mine calls them "scholarships for poor kids." With voucher money, parents can send their children to whatever school they choose—or they can home school—which also requires money.

Alternative Schooling

Most school districts have many alternative schools. Alternative schools have a certain focus—maybe they are for the arts or rigorous college prep schools or something else. Those schools however don't necessarily mean better education. There are private schools. Private schools often do with less money a better job than our well-funded public schools. They also usually don't waste time with subjects that aren't academic. Then, there is home schooling. About 1.8 million students (3%) are presently home schooled. Those students often take national honors in the "BEES"—Spelling Bees and Geography Bees. These students have the advantage of being able to go through the material as fast as they wish. Also, they can take the foreign language of their choice through several venues.

The average ACT score has sloped downward recently, but some students still manage to get a perfect score. It's rare, but it happens. The most recent is Joshua Owens of Louisiana. When asked to explain his secret, he said "homeschooling." He commented: "Home schooling gave me an advantage because the instruction is tailored for the individual."[1]

My friend and neighbor home schooled her son from 5th grade on. She was not a teacher herself, and when he was taking Calculus, Chemistry, Physics, etc., it was totally up to her son. He got up and got going in the morning and got his work out and put on the video (VHS in those days) and watched it until he understood the material and did the problems and reading work connected with it. After he finished his high school curriculum, he walked right into Colorado School of Mines and graduated in four years with straight "A"s and was number one in his class. He is probably an unusual case, but it is possible.

Home schooling seems like a radical idea—but only because we are conditioned to think of it that way. Why? Because most of us attended school. But, after several overhauls of our public education system in less than 30 years, the schools aren't getting the job done.

Many of us feel inadequate to take on the responsibility of homeschooling. The curricula you can buy packaged and complete for each grade level are wonderful. The one I used for my children was Calvert, out of Baltimore, MD. Calvert is the oldest home school curricula in the country and was used very far back by missionaries who were sent to places like Africa. They took their families, so this met their need. The big box contains everything needed—pencils, books, teacher's manuals, paper, tests,

etc. I have also heard great things about Abeka. The only shortcoming that I found with Calvert with my son, who was in 3rd grade and loved math, was that he was ahead of the math they had in the curriculum. So I got him a Saxon Math book which he loved and finished it even though it was for 5th or 6th graders.

I can hear you thinking, "But I still want my student to be 'socialized'." They need not lose out on socialization. There are other avenues. I only home schooled my son one school year (3rd) and my daughter for two (7th and 8th), but in the evening they had Tae Kwan Do lessons, soccer practice, and piano lessons. And our daughter also had ballet lessons. They really didn't miss anything, and felt they learned much. Our daughter, because of the extensive grammar regimen with Calvert, has near-perfect grammar and did all the writing for her employer (a national home mortgage company) since she wrote so much better than her boss did. I only got a taste of home school, but I saw its advantages. Also, some high schools partner with home schoolers.

As you can see, I have a bias toward home schooling (but only as a result of the failure of our public schools). There are some good elementary, middle, and high schools, but they have to be sought after ardently. Make sure the values and philosophy imbibed at school don't undermine what your student is being taught at home. It sets up a great conflict. Of course you have to make sure the academic rigor part of the search has been satisfied. In my opinion we need a back-to-basics movement in schools that emphasizes facts. Students also need to be taught the work ethic. Our highest priority should be to cultivate their intellect using core curricula and great

works of literature. After that they will be outfitted in the best way to make excellent decisions in their lives, in their lines of work, in their communities, and in their marriages/homes. I don't see changes happening in our public schools in time for this generation, unfortunately. Therefore I'm suggesting home school for your consideration.

Another great article in the *Wall Street Journal* from the Week End Edition, January 20 and 21, 2018, entitled "A Very Bad Bargain," talks about the effect of collective bargaining (the Unions). A Cornell study says students suffer from collective bargaining. It has to do with how teachers' collective bargaining affects students' employment and earnings later in life. They conclude that there is strong evidence that teacher collective bargaining has a negative effect on students' earnings as adults. Given that 34 states since 1959 have mandated collective bargaining with teachers and only seven prohibit it, the finding is also a call to reform.

The study compares outcomes of students from collective bargaining states with outcomes of students from states without collective bargaining. It adjusts for such aspects as black, Hispanic, white, and male/female. Students who spent all 12 years of their elementary and secondary education in schools with mandatory collective bargaining, earned $795 less per year as adults than their peers who weren't in such schools. They also worked an average of a half hour less per week, were 0.9% less likely to be employed, and were in occupations requiring lower skills. The authors found that these add up to a large overall loss of $196 billion per year of students educated in the 34 states with mandated collective bargaining.

We must resist the inclination to help our kids too much. Lots of us are averse to seeing our children fail or struggle at something, but wisdom often comes to us through failure. Any successful man/woman will say his success came from lots of failures. It toughens our children; instructs them and betters them. (But we all know that there are some circumstances where this is inappropriate. We all have to be the judge of that.) Did you know that if you help a baby chick who is pecking its shell that it probably won't survive? It's too weak. It needs the strength afforded by the effort of pecking. Einstein said "There is only one road to human greatness: through the school of hard knocks."

The Need for More Foreign Language

There was a very interesting article in the *Washington Times* by Alex Zietlow weighing in on the subject of foreign language education. It was in the Thursday, June 15, 2017, edition. "The inability of too many Americans to learn to speak anything but English constitutes a foreign language 'emergency' that could end up harming the economy and impairing U.S. foreign policy. ... Only 20.7% of American adults can speak a foreign language, compared with 66% of all European adults. ... We risk being left out of any conversation that does not take place in English. ...Proficiency in a foreign language can translate into employment opportunities. ... We should treat language education as a persistent national need like competency in math or English." Many of our high schools today only offer one or two foreign languages due to lack of interest. Also, the absence of foreign language requirements may shed light on the dropping scores. Studies show that those who learn a second language

111

demonstrate higher achievement in the areas of math, science, and reading.

The Mother Tongue

Far from being adequate at a foreign language, many of our students don't even speak English well. *The Mother Tongue* is the name of a very good book, but it is a real thing as well. Children learn English from their parents— mostly from their mothers who are with them all the time. If she speaks English well, her children will too. And what the students learn in English class in school just reinforces their proficiency.

This, however, doesn't seem to be the case today. Many adults don't speak correctly because they weren't taught correctly either. That gets passed down to their children. We have personal friends who are a perfect example. The husband and wife are wonderful people, but they both use poor English. The husband is in insurance, and we have known for a while that he has been looking for better work—a better company and something more lucrative. We'll call him Ted. Ted routinely gets to the final stages of applying because of his strong resume and his great track record of sales. The companies then set up personal interviews—usually with the top three applicants. Ted always makes it to this stage, but I feel sure his poor grammar usage gets noticed in a face-to-face meeting, and he always loses out. Ted and his wife have passed down their grammar to their children. School English classes are inadequate to correct them. A life-long habit is really hard to break.

Reinstating Speech Classes

A few years ago schools had something called speech classes. Students prepared speeches on some topic that interested them and then presented them in front of the rest of the class. The teacher critiqued the speeches right then and there—what they did well, what words they mispronounced, how they built their speech—introduction, body, conclusion. Lots of good help! Everyone got to hear. They all knew it would be their turn pretty soon, so they listened carefully.

I remember my speech class in 7th grade. I used the word "genuine" in it. I pronounced it wrong, and got corrected. I have said it correctly ever since—glad to know the right way! This type of class would satisfy so many needs. The students would learn interesting information, the desire to "perform" in front of the class would be met, and they would learn the correct pronunciation of certain words plus have their grammar straightened out—all in a happy, friendly, setting!

David McCullough talks about a verbal virus. He has a wonderful new book called *The American Spirit* where he says to teachers: "Please, please, do what you can to cure the verbal virus that seems increasingly rampant...I am talking about the relentless, wearisome use of the words 'like' and 'you know' and 'awesome' and 'actually.' Listen to yourselves as you speak. Just imagine if, in his inaugural address John F. Kennedy had said, 'Ask not what your country can, you know, do for you, but what you can, like, do for your country actually.'"[2]

Hand Written Notes

In a paper entitled "Phenomenology of the Hand" by Mark Bauerlein, he tells us about the connection of the hand to the brain. Students who take notes by hand and then transcribe them again by hand, seem to learn the material better and retain it better. Quoting Mr. Bauerlein: "Students write faster with keyboard and mouse, but would anybody say that student writing has improved in the last three decades? Certainly the test scores say no. The SAT added a writing component in 2005, and scores have gone down every year except two of them, when they were flat. The ACT college readiness scores in English have dropped six points in the last five years (67 percent of test takers reached readiness in 2012, 61 percent in 2016.) With all the tools available to amend grammar and usage and spelling, twenty-first-century students aren't gaining. They are writing more words than ever before, yes, but because of social media, more hasn't meant better. ... The keyboard isn't an advance on the pen. It's a step sideways, if not backward."[3]

Teachers

We have a certain opinion about teachers. Usually it is good, and deservedly so, but not always. In the movie *Waiting for Superman,* a statistic was pointed out that in no other profession is it so hard to fire someone who has been hired. One in 97 lawyers loses his/her law license per year; one in 57 doctors. For teachers; one in 2500 loses his/her teaching license (certificate). The teachers' unions have done a good job of protecting their members.

There are those who are holding the reins of power in education who do not look at educating the students the way I do, and, I hope the way most Americans see education. Let me quote from a couple.

This is H.L. Mencken in *The American Mercury* in April 1924: The aim of public education is not: "...to fill the young of the species with knowledge and awaken their intelligence...Nothing could be further from the truth. The aim...is simply to reduce as many individuals as possible to the same safe level, to breed and train a standardized citizenry, to put down dissent and originality. This is its aim in the United States."

Did you know that the teachers' unions don't have our children's best interest at heart either? Actually it all makes sense. A union is a fiduciary of its members. In that light this statement is logical. Albert Shanker, President of the National Federation of Teachers (NFT) said this: "When students start paying dues, we'll start paying attention to their interests."[4]

Teachers' unions have taken the position not to distinguish among teachers. Therefore they cannot sanction merit pay. The NEA membership is three million. (Did you know that teachers' unions give the most to political causes—more than the Teamsters or the NRA combined? And it's nearly all to one party.)

Recent New Jersey Revelation

Project Veritas caught on camera President Dr. David Perry of the Hamilton Township Education Association saying to a woman, "I am here to defend even the worst teachers." He also said that he would lie to protect the teachers and the teacher's union.[5]

SCREENS—Cell Phones, Computers, TV

Revisiting the subject of cell phones: it has been stated that with a cell phone we hold in our hand more technology than NASA had when they put a man on the moon. It is astounding. The cell phone is a computer you hold in your hand. I remember working in Boston the summer of 1964 and visiting MIT. The school had one of the first computers—housed in an entire building. They jokingly said that one of the main uses it had been put to was randomizing the color of the upholstery on the seats in the school auditorium. (They were purple, turquoise, and pink.) Truly it is a miracle, and we should be so grateful. As for the cell phone, in a second we can ask Siri for a piece of information it might take many minutes to locate otherwise. That convenience is addictive! But it has to be managed.

The *Wall Street Journal* had an article January 2, 2016 entitled "Teach Your Children Well: Unhook Them from Technology." One of the parents in this kind of school (Waldorf Schools) recalls putting her son in front of the TV when he was a toddler while she did her chores. "It wasn't until he started kindergarten that she understood that the screen time was hurting his ability to entertain himself, to enjoy books and even to like playing outside." Jennifer McMillan, a teacher at a school that operates with this philosophy, says that many parents simply don't understand the effects that staring at a screen can have on children's behavior and their ability to learn. Research backs this up: in December, 2015, the *Journal of the American Medical Association*, "JAMA," published a study that showed that electronic toys hindered verbal development. I know a man who experienced this first

hand in trying to carry on a conversation with a young man who couldn't even look him in the eye. The book *Disconnected* gives a lot more detail of the detrimental aspect of screen time, and especially social media. The art of looking things up in books should still be taught. There may come a time when our smartphone isn't handy.

But, before I leave this subject, I just came across the latest information about a new app. Social media is so huge to our children. This app. is called the "HONESTY APP." Remember when there were the "most likely to succeed, best smile, cutest couple" questions that were usually connected with the high school year book? No more. Now there is a new breed of massively popular apps. targeted to teens to let them poll one another on everything from their popularity to a new pair of shoes. These apps. are designed to deliver the message anonymously. Honesty app. users can pose questions such as "am I pretty?" and get many many brutally "honest" answers—with no ability to reply. They can't even block the one who sent the reply.[6] Another great reason for a dumb phone!

Learning by Stories

We must pass on the torch of cultural literacy. I'm talking about the famous and beautiful literature, the allusions to which we see in all kinds of writing. And they often go over the kids' heads. The fact that this heritage is not being passed on with all its zest—and marvelous stories— is probably the reason I see such apathy in the current generation—lack of beautiful, exciting tales. A book called *The Story Killers* by Terrance O. Moore, addresses that subject—that children learn by stories.

A Startling Quote

Bryan Caplan, an Economist from George Mason University, has an article entitled "The Case Against Education." In it he says the education system is a waste of time and money. He says "I love education too much to accept its Orwellian substitute."[7]

CHAPTER 9

How Did We Get Here?

How did this deterioration of our schools happen and we didn't notice? As I have said before, when your student seems to be doing well at school you don't feel alarmed. There are things that have happened to "throw off" our sense of how school is performing.

There has been a philosophy pervading education counter to the educational philosophy that existed in the '50s. Beginning with the 1960s, we've seen a remarkable change: a general moral degradation. I believe our culture is under assault. We now have freedom-killing political correctness. There have been those with different ideas about what education is that have gained control over the various teacher associations. They have met with little resistance since modifications were slight and gradual. There has been a drift away from what was generally thought of as an educated intellect. Some of these basics have been supplanted, or the time delegated to them shortened, to provide for teaching other ideas.

"Millennials now make up the largest generation in America, and we're seeing some deeply worrisome

trends," said Marion Smith, executive director for the Victims of Communism, according to *Market Watch*. "Millennials are increasingly turning away from capitalism and toward socialism and even communism as a viable alternative."[1] The findings of this study should be a wake-up call to those who think communism is no longer a threat to the United States and the West. Young people have had little personal experience with the half-century battle between Soviet tyranny and American freedom. Marxism (Communism) is plainly stated as taking from one group and giving it to another group—that it is fair, equitable, and compassionate. People are being led to believe that's a good thing! The famous economist, Milton Friedman, said, "A society that puts equality before freedom will get neither. A society that puts freedom before equality will get a higher degree of both."[2] Winston Churchill's famous quote is perfect here, "The main vice of capitalism is the uneven distribution of prosperity. The main vice of socialism is the even distribution of misery."[3]

Nikita Khrushchev said "You Americans are so gullible. No, you won't accept communism outright, but we'll keep feeding you small doses of socialism until you'll finally wake up and find you already have communism. We won't have to fight you. We'll so weaken your economy until you'll fall like overripe fruit into our hands."

One might say that Khrushchev was wrong since the Soviet Union broke up in 1989. But there are more worldwide self-declared communists today then there were then. Check out "The Communist Party USA" on Google.

A few years ago I viewed a documentary film called *AGENDA*. It affected me greatly. Because of that film I read three books that have enlightened me—more than that, they made my jaw drop. One was *The Naked Communist*, by Cleon Skousen, a former FBI agent. It was written in 1958 and contained a list of 45 goals that those of the Communist world had made to help take down the United States. (By the way, these goals were read into the Congressional Record in 1963.) I will quote number 17 of the 45 goals since it relates to education: "Get control of the schools. Use them as transmission belts for socialism and current Communist propaganda. Soften the curriculum. Get control of teacher's associations. Put the party line in textbooks."[4]

People who hold the communist ideal believe whole heartedly that their way of governance is best and should be used throughout the world. And indeed I am old enough to remember when the world was divided into what was called the "Communist World" and the "Free World." The Communists had plans to bring the entire world under their ideology, starting on other continents, and that the United States would be last to change because of certain strengths. (It is hard for me to think of a people who would wish ill on me or on my country.)

Antonio Gramsci said the way to destroy the West was to destroy its culture. The story of Whitaker Chambers, who defected to the west, related in the book, *The Naked Communist,* was shocking. He was Moscow's primary agent in the United States. When he defected he helped to identify many communists in our government, all the while his own life was in grave danger because of his

defection. He said: "Communism succeeds because most people who support communism aren't communists."

The next book was J. Edgar Hoover's *Masters of Deceit*. Since he knew of these cases first-hand (being the head of the FBI), he had many examples of people operating in our country who were ready at a moment's notice to leave wife, children, home, and job (maybe forever) to further "The Cause."

The last book was *None Dare Call it Treason* by John Stormer. He was just a private citizen who started doing his own research. When he had written his book, no publisher would publish it since he was an unknown author. So he had to publish it himself. He sold them out of his garage. In those days (1964) there weren't credit cards or PayPal. It was cash or check. He mailed them out of his garage. The books he sold numbered in the millions. In it he argues that America was losing the Cold War due to domestic communism.

I don't believe that there could have been such a radical and harmful change to our society and our educational system if it had simply been just left to the natural maturation of a society. If you want a reality check, watch a few of the old movies and see how people behaved and how they looked and how they spoke. If this trend is successful, it will destroy the greatest country in all world history. Joseph Stalin said: "America is like a healthy body and its resistance is three fold: its patriotism, its morality, and its spiritual life. If we can undermine these three areas, America will collapse from within." Vladimir Lenin said "The goal of Socialism is Communism."

"Social justice" is a new term that has recently come into use, but it is a buzz phrase for socialism. (Its real definition is redistribution of outcomes.) Social justice as taught in schools doesn't mean justice as we understand it. There has been a revolution without our ever knowing about it. Willi Munsenberg said: "We are going to make the West so corrupt it stinks." Ronald Reagan reminded us that: "Freedom is never more than one generation away from extinction."

We grew up with more prosperity than any people in human history, so it seems incredible that people would turn on the system that gave it to them. We have prosperous utopians! They don't know the dangers of utopia—and that the idea itself is an opiate. Our youth know nothing except decades of unchallenged international supremacy, and these Americans have let their guards down to real threats to our way of life—if their guards ever were up. There is a general false sense of security about our future. There are dangerous doctrines that they (and we) have had the good fortune to escape, that are being considered for acceptance again. We are losing our ability to call evil, evil. Our students are being taught not to be judgmental—but we have to make good judgments! Patrick Moore, Co-Founder of Green Peace, quit his own movement when he realized it had been captured by the environmentalists (which is seen as an arm of the Communist Party U.S.A.), because it was the only vehicle that could create enough red tape to slow our economy. The Hammer and Sickle should invoke the same contempt as the Swastika. Stalin killed even more people than Hitler.

Mao starved 60 to 80 million of his people to buy armaments from Russia. When people are starving they don't get hungry and drop dead. It's very ugly.

Today in Venezuela the people are starving in the streets. They have broken into the Caracas Zoo to steal and eat the animals which are starving too. "Venezuela's inflation rate topped 40,000 percent."[5] Venezuela is an oil-rich country!

About two years ago I heard a talk by a young man from Sweden who is in the U.S. going to college. He'd just been home for Christmas break, and he was so disheartened by what he saw. He said Sweden is going bankrupt. He told us it would take about three more years and there would be no more money. Sweden is known for its generosity— in fact it is called a multicultural utopia, but its reserves are about to be used up because of its generosity. He said his family would like to emigrate to the U.S., but they lack a sponsor.

Finland had a "free money" experiment that began in January 2017—free healthcare and free college. The government is ending it at the end of this year (2018). Carter McClung, University of Texas M.A. Economics, pointed out, "Designing good incentive structures for 'free' things is very hard. When things are free, people start behaving strangely. … We are all familiar with an all you can eat buffet! Societies (likewise) tend to overuse services which are free or under costed." The *New York Times* said, "Now the experiment is ending. The Finish government has opted not to continue financing it past this year, a reflection of public discomfort with the idea of dispensing government largess free of requirements that

its recipients seek work."[6]   They have long practiced Democratic Socialism.

Capitalism has been adopted by China and its economy is flourishing, but its people aren't free because their government is still communist. Students, in their desire for more freedom, protested in Tiananmen Square many years ago. They were pushing forward a replica of the Statue of Liberty. It was a peaceful protest, but the tanks ran them down anyway. Even today a Chinese citizen can be arrested by any police officer and sent away to a "Reeducation Through Labor Camp" for two years without any due process at all. (Capitalism has lifted more people out of poverty than any other system.)

Count those people (teachers) as unfaithful stewards who don't warn students of a known threat. A favorable opinion of "Big Government" – Totalitarianism (Socialism, Nazism, Fascism, Communism, etc.) is now in the ascendency in our schools. Many students like it, and they aren't being corrected by teachers with solid information about its dangers. There is ample historical evidence of the dangers and harms of socialism and communism— whether it be Hitler's National Socialism (Nazism) or Stalin's Soviet Socialism (Union of Soviet Socialist Republics—USSR). I overheard some 10th graders talking about how great socialism was working in Europe.

A visual of communism's ability to prevent prosperity is a quick glance at an earth view from a satellite at night. Look at North Korea, where communism holds its people in the tightest grip. It is dark. There are no lights emanating from it. There is no prosperity there.

From a Young Woman at Harvard

A young woman, Laura M. Nicolae, a student at Harvard in the class of 2020 is an applied mathematics major. She recently shared in the *CRIMSON* the story of how her father arrived in the United States. She titled her message to her fellow students: "Think Twice Before Embracing Communism." Now I am quoting from her.

> "In 1988, my twenty-six-year-old father jumped off a train in the middle of Hungary with nothing but the clothes on his back. For the next two years, he fled an oppressive Romanian Communist regime that would kill him if they ever laid hands on him again.

> "My father ran from a government that beat, tortured, and brainwashed its citizens. His childhood friend disappeared after scrawling an insult about the dictator on the school bathroom wall. His neighbors starved to death from food rations designed to combat 'obesity.' As the population dwindled, women were sent to the hospital every month to make sure they were getting pregnant.

> "Walk around campus, and you're likely to spot Ché Guevara on a few shirts and button pins. A sophomore jokes that he's declared a secondary major in 'communist ideology and implementation.' The New Leftist Club on campus seeks 'a modern perspective' on Marx and Lenin to 'alleviate the stigma around the concept of leftism.' An author laments in these pages that it's too difficult to meet communists here. For many

students, casually endorsing communism is a cool, edgy way to gripe about the world. The world has yet to witness a benevolent communist state.

> "Communism cannot be separated from oppression; in fact, it depends upon it. One would think that the idea that Russia's brutal Communist state was simply the 'illegitimate child' of Marxism and would be dead, considering the track record of the regimes that followed. But ideas die hard— unless you've endured and suffered from their consequences."[7]

Aleksandr Solzhenitsyn commented that "For Russia communism is a dead dog. For many people in the West, it is still a living lion."

I will close by quoting from a book by Cleon Skousen: *The Five Thousand Year Leap.* People in Europe in the early 1800s were puzzled about America. No one there had believed the "American Experiment" would work. The form of government the Founders came up with was too different from any known governing system. Yet they had heard that America was thriving, the people were happy, the cities were pretty, and commerce was good. Alexis de Tocqueville, a French aristocrat, decided to come see for himself. He spent three years. Here is a quote from the book:

> "I sought for the greatness and genius of America in her commodious harbors and her ample rivers, and it was not there; in her fertile fields and boundless prairies, and it was not there; in her rich mines and her vast world commerce, and it was not there. Not until I went to the churches of America and heard her pulpits

aflame with righteousness did I understand the secret of her genius and power. America is great because she is good, and if America ever ceases to be good, America will cease to be great."[8]

Thanks for reading my book. If you want to follow up on any of this, and you only have time for one thing, look at the movie *AGENDA*.

Recommended Reading and Viewing

Books:

1776 – David McCullough
The American Spirit – David McCullough
The Naked Communist – W. Cleon Skousen (especially pp. 259—262)
Masters of Deceit – J. Edgar Hoover
None Dare Call It Treason – John Stormer
The 5000 Year Leap – W. Cleon Skousen
Dumbing Us Down – John Taylor Gatto
Not With My Child, You Don't – Robert Holland
Child Abuse in the Classroom – Phyllis Schlafly
America the Beautiful – Ben Carson
The Teacher Who Couldn't Read – John Corcoran
The War Against Grammar – David Mulroy
The American Miracle – Michael Medved
The Story Killers – Terrance O. Moore
Why Johnny Can't Read – Rudolf Flesch
Why Johnny Still Can't Read (25 years later) – Rudolf Flesch
Disconnected – Thomas Kersting
Your Teacher Said What? – Joe and Blake Kernen
Dumbing Down Our Kids – Charles J. Sykes

DVDs

AGENDA and AGENDA 2 – Both by Curtis Bowers
A More Perfect Union
Waiting for Superman
Stand and Deliver
The Girl Who Spelled Freedom
The Enemies Within

APPENDIX

A Great Math Series

Some math books are better than others, but a really good series is the Saxon Math Series. The beauty of these books is that they are self-explanatory. By that I mean that there is a paragraph at the top of each lesson (the book is composed of "lessons" and not divided into chapters) that explains the day's lesson. It explains it so well, that no teacher is needed for the most part. John Saxon wrote a masterful series. By the way, not only were his "word problems" interesting and appropriate, but he included in them information from history and geography and even English literature. He was intentionally teaching on several levels.

Cultural Literacy Taught Even in Cartoons in Earlier Days

Even cartoons in the earlier days taught cultural literacy. The artists of the cartoons we saw at movie theatres before the feature started had a desire for their work not only to be entertaining but also educational—though we didn't know it. The themes they sometimes chose were great literature using great music. Most of these cartoons were produced by Warner Brothers. There was a cartoon version of *A Connecticut Yankee in King Arthur's Court*. Even if the kids never read that book, they knew the story. Bugs Bunny was used in Robert Louis Stevenson's *Strange Case of Dr. Jekyll and Mr. Hyde*. There was something called *The Cat Concerto* with famous music; and also The *Rabbit of Saville*. Children greatly benefited from these cultural literacy lessons they never knew they had! If they encountered these stories or music later in school or in life they would be familiar.

Examples of the Necessity of Striving

I recently read a magazine article about a gentleman who, when taking a walk, came upon a caterpillar where the butterfly inside was trying to get out. He could see the struggle inside. He took his pocket knife and made a tiny hole at the bottom so that the butterfly could enlarge it and free itself. As he watched, it did just that and it fell to the ground. The front part of its wings was fully developed, but the back part wasn't, and was shriveled. It ran across the ground and didn't fly. The rest of the wing structure needed to have the fluid pumped into them to unfurl those wings. He was so sorry he'd interfered.

One more example: You may remember that scientists created a completely enclosed artificial environment called Biosphere 2 in Arizona and made one mistake that caused all the trees to fall down before maturing. There was no wind, so trees didn't develop stress wood, which is necessary for them to stand.

Man on the Street Interviews

You may have heard some of these interviews conducted by Jesse Watters, Jay Leno, etc. These were easy questions asked to random people on the streets of New York City. Most of the ones being questioned were college students. The answers to their questions seemed like a joke, but they were not. Here are three: "Who did the South fight in the Civil War?" The answer was, "North Korea;" "Who did America declare its independence from?" The answer was, "Virginia;" "What year did we declare our independence?" The answer was, "1984." If you are not familiar with these man-on-the-street interviews, they're accessible on Google.

Reading

Teaching reading right away at the beginning of elementary school is so very important. A child's ability or inability to read can color his concept of himself and school. And "Phonics" should be the medium, in my opinion. John Corcoran, from California, visited Denver in 2012 to speak at the Independence Institute about READING. He, himself did not read until age 48—and this man was a teacher! John Corcoran's first book that he wrote after his wonderful experience of learning to read was *The Teacher Who Couldn't Read*. His story was so remarkable that he'd been on Oprah. Before he began his talk to us, he played that Oprah clip. It's an engaging book and I urge you to read it. He was finally taught Phonics at 48, and he said "The weight of the world dropped off my shoulders." He had spent his whole life up to that point hiding the fact he couldn't read.

His second book was a research work. He went to most of the male prisons in the country and did interviews and created a survey. He found 70% of the incarcerated men couldn't read. His goal was to get teachers to teach phonics and to keep working with students until they could read.

FOOTNOTES

Chapter 1

1. Please google: Michael Hairston Fairfax Education Association Cursive
2. The Wall Street Journal, August, 29, 2018, p. A17

Chapter 2

1. Please google: Mary Mackie, what everybody ought to know about band
2. Please google: middle school teacher in Ft. Wayne, Indiana says boy can't use Fox news story

Chapter 3

1. *The American Miracle*, Michael Medved, pp. 85, 86
2. *The Teacher Who Couldn't Read*, John Corcoran, p. 20
3. Please google: 2017 New York teacher taught genderbread
4. Please google: Orange County Board of Education says parents cannot opt students out of sex education
5. Please google: Ames Iowa marching band won't play national anthem
6. Please google: California High School banned National Anthem at pep rallies
7. Please google: Virginia school Muslim calligraphy there is no god but Allah

8   Please google: Canopy Oaks Elementary special pronouns

9   Please google: Salk Elementary Declaration of Independence

10 Please google: Dyer County, Tennessee senior girl suspended bless you

11 Please google: the sneeze at graduation

12 Please google: Hampton Middle School, Georgia teacher told students to write letters for stricter gun controls.

Chapter 4

1. Wall Street Journal, August 11, 2017, A 13

2. Please google: Tennessee high school students not fulfilling requirements

3. Please google: Nations Report Card begs US to get back to basics.

4. Please google: UNC reading specialist to resign

5. Please google: Richard Vedder Ohio Univ. Center for College Affordability and Productivity

Chapter 5

1. *Disconnected*, Thomas Kersting, p. 8

2. Please google: schools and computers don't mix

Chapter 6

1. Please google: in 1995 SAT changed

2. Please google: College Board 2015 revised test negative about America
3. Please look at the 2019 edition of the AP US History Textbook
4. Please google: How America did on the PISA test in 2015
5. *The Underground History of American Education*, John Taylor Gatto, p. xvi

Chapter 7

1. Please google: Springfield College purges men in literature
2. Please google: Trinity College Johnny Eric Williams white people inhuman
3. Please google: ACTA President Anne Neal says American Universities don't love Shakespeare
4. Please google: University of Pennsylvania removes Shakespeare's portrait
5. Please google: University of California Davis lists gender neutral pronouns
6. *An Unauthorized Biography of Jordan B. Peterson, by Richard West, p.28*
7. Please google: Arizona State University professor lets students organize anti-Trump rally
8. Please google: Columbia University demanding less Eurocentric reading
9. Please google: Yale University can't print F. Scott Fitzgerald quote

10. Please google: Smith College doesn't like Huckelberry Finn
11. Please google: L. Todd Wood the Air Force Academy doesn't train warriors any more
12. Please google: University of Northern Colorado basketball team stripped of title
13. Please google: Ulrich Baer of New York Univ. defended shutting down speech
14. Please google: *Communist Manifesto* common on campuses
15. Please google: history departments don't require American history
16. Fox News, Tucker Carlson Show, May 25, 2018
17. The *Weekly Standard*, April 30, 2018, p. 3 (reprinted from the *Washington Post*)

Chapter 8

1. Please google: Joshua Owens perfect score on ACT
2. *The American Spirit*, David McCullough, p. 148
3. Please google: Mark Bauerlein hand written notes
4. Please google: Albert Shanker when students pay dues we will start paying attention to their interests
5. Please google: Dr. David Perry Hamilton Township I will defend the worst teachers
6. Please google: honesty app on phones
7. Please google: Bryan Caplan George Mason Univ. case against education

Chapter 9

1. Please google: Marion Smith Market Watch millennials turning away from capitalism
2. Please google: Milton Friedman a society that puts equality before freedom will get neither
3. Please google: Winston Churchill capitalism the uneven distribution of prosperity
4. The *Naked Communist*, Cleon Skousen, p 260
5. Please google: Venezuela 40,000 percent inflation
6. Please google: Finland free money experiment
7. Please google: Young Woman at Harvard writes about Communism
8. *The 5000 Year Leap; A Miracle That Changed the World*, Cleon Skousen, p. 84

Made in the USA
Columbia, SC
06 January 2019